*In Trying Times,*
# JUST KEEP
# TRYING!

OTHER TITLES BY
MERRILEE BOYACK

*52 Weeks of Fun Family Service*

*How Do I Change My Husband?* (talk on CD)

*The Parenting Breakthrough: A Real-Life Plan to Teach Your Kids
to Work, Save Money, and Be Truly Independent*

*Teaching Your Children to Fly: A Guide to Independence*
(talk on CD)

*Toss the Guilt and Catch the Joy: A Woman's Guide to a Better Life*

*Strangling Your Husband Is Not an Option: A Practical Guide to
Dramatically Improving Your Marriage*

# *In Trying Times,*
# JUST KEEP
# TRYING!

## MERRILEE BOYACK

DESERET
BOOK

SALT LAKE CITY, UTAH

**Library of Congress Cataloging-in-Publication Data**

Boyack, Merrilee Browne.
    In trying times, just keep trying! / Merrilee Boyack.
        p. cm.
    Includes bibliographical references.
    ISBN 978-1-60641-597-9 (paperbound)
    1. Suffering—Religious aspects—Church of Jesus Christ of Latter-day Saints. 2. Christian life—Mormon authors.   3. Church of Jesus Christ of Latter-day Saints—Doctrines. 4. Boyack, Merrilee Browne.   I. Title.
    BX8643.S93B68 2010
    248.8'6—dc22                                                    2009046673

Printed in the United States of America
R. R. Donnelley, Crawfordsville, IN

10    9    8    7    6    5    4    3    2    1

*To Pat Williams and Carolyn Rasmus,*
*who saved my life through a quirky turn of events.*
*Thanks, sisters!*

# Contents

*Contents*

## Chapter 8
*Choosing to Celebrate the Good*

## Chapter 9
*Choosing to Let Go and Heal*

## Chapter 10
*Choosing to Move Forward*

# Preface

I'm in the middle of it. There's no doubt about it. Now you and I both know that books are usually written at the *end* of it. The author will say, "Oh, I made it through! And I learned so much!" They relate how the whole experience was wrapped up with a nice tidy bow. They extol the lessons learned, the blessings received, and the progress made. At the end. Clearly at the end. When it's all done. . . .

I'm not at the end. Yes, I've learned lessons, received blessings, and made some progress, but I have no idea when it will all end. I'm just hoping some of it will end soon. My prayers are often now just that the bad stuff will slow down. That would be blessing enough.

So if you're going to read a book by someone who is in the middle of it, I should probably give you some warnings. First, this book is personal. I'll be sharing many things that I'm going through, both as an individual and with my family. If you don't like that kind of book, stop reading, and regift this without any guilt. Second, this book is not all perky and humorous. I normally have quite a sense of humor and I hope that will still come through, but you have to know that it's taken a hit. I'll try hard not to be too depressing—in fact, I hope ultimately to be encouraging—but there's some sad and hard stuff that will be discussed. That's OK. We're all going through sad and hard stuff. And if not now, shortly. Third, some of these things don't have nice, neat answers. There is no tidy bow at the end. That's OK, too. I think we rarely (and maybe never) hit a point in life where all the questions are answered.

For the brave who choose to continue to read along and join me in the journey, I welcome you. We shall learn and hope and pray and ask questions together. And if you are touched by just one thing about this story, the experience will have been worth it.

Feel free to send me an e-mail about your own experience at maboyack@gmail.com or my Web site at Boyacks.com/Merrilee.

CHAPTER 1

# Facing the Storms of Life

It's been a year. An unbelievable year. I was talking to a friend recently and she said, "Who would have ever believed so much would have happened in the last year?" I replied that if I'd known, I would have gone to bed and pulled the covers over my head and taken a pass on the whole thing!

A year ago I was racing through my life having a great time. It was a crazy life, I admit. I have four adult sons and five part-time jobs. Two of my boys were still living at home. I was serving as the Relief Society president—for the second time in the same ward—as well. I was also lecturing weekly and traveling all over the country often. It was so much fun!

The summer was really going by fast. I serve on the city council for my city and was in the middle of a busy re-election campaign running for my second term.

Then I heard the news. I live in Southern California and the Protect Marriage Amendment (Proposition 8), favoring traditional marriage, had qualified to be on the fall ballot. I knew what that meant.

Nine years prior, I had served as the area coordinator for Proposition 22, coordinating the efforts in my area to pass the traditional marriage law. It had been an incredible and incredibly difficult experience. And I knew this time it would be significantly harder. And I knew that I would be asked to help again. So night after night, I sat in my rocking chair on my back porch and just wept. I could feel the freight train coming.

Sure enough, a few weeks later a meeting was called and I was asked to attend to give everyone an organizational framework from my past experience. At the end of the meeting, a counselor in the stake presidency said, "So, Merrilee, what are you up to now?"

I recounted that I was campaigning, working on a book, traveling, speaking, and oh, yeah, I was Relief Society president. He and the committee were shocked.

He said, "Wow, you really don't have time to do this, do you?"

"No, I really don't," I replied. "But if you ask me, I will say yes."

He looked me in the eye and said, "We're asking."

Now this was one of those moments where you have to mentally think, "*Hold* it. Just hold it in. Do *not* fall apart now. Just hang on." And I did.

I said yes, of course, and held in my emotions all the way to the parking lot. Then the tears came. (Frankly, I've done a lot of crying in parking lots this year. I've come to look upon them with fondness. They are such wonderful, comforting places of anonymity and privacy where you can just let it all out.)

I flew out the next morning to speak at BYU–Idaho Education Week. As I was driving to Rexburg from the airport in Utah, I prayed mightily. I longed to have a deep confirmation that this new assignment was the Lord's will in my life. I mean, I knew it was coming. I just wanted to *know.* After hours of driving and praying, the confirmation came. This was my next assignment. I knew it without a doubt.

And then life really began to speed up. As the regional coordinator for the Protect Marriage Amendment, I was organizing hundreds and thousands of volunteers. We distributed more than eight thousand yard signs from my house and more than sixty thousand pieces of literature.

The hard parts hit as well. Early in the process, we had set up a Web site that became quite the focal point for outrage throughout the country. I began to be deluged with daily e-mails from all kinds of people from all throughout the area and state and country. And many of them—perhaps even most of them—were not kind. It became very painful day after day to wade through the work that was required of me and to keep my chin up and spine strong. Thousands of e-mails were going out almost on a daily basis. I was receiving hundreds of e-mails in return. The messages were averaging about two per minute. Sometimes I would just sit there and watch them pop up. And every single one of them had to be answered.

Let's be honest. The work was scary. No one wanted to go door-to-door. No one wanted to stand on street corners with political signs and have drivers "point the finger of scorn" (1 Nephi 8:33) at them. (Lehi and Nephi were right on the mark with that one.) But I also drew strength from the many volunteers who demonstrated their amazing courage on a daily basis. I have seen more faithfulness and valiance and devotion in the last year than I have in a lifetime.

The days were crazy. One minute sending out an e-mail to

several thousand people. The next minute answering a phone call from a sister in the ward who was in distress. Then helping my son apply for college. Then preparing a speech for my campaign. Then drafting documents for a client. On and on it went. I was at my breaking point.

But I knew a joyful couple of days were coming. I had been asked to speak at one of several Time Out for Women events. One event had been scheduled for Anchorage, Alaska. Oh, how I wanted to go! I had been to forty-nine states; Alaska was my last one. My friend Carolyn Rasmus, who was scheduled to go to Alaska, graciously agreed that we could switch assignments. I was so excited!

Alaska is a beautiful state! It was so wonderful, and I enjoyed a peaceful couple of days, relaxing and sightseeing and visiting with the wonderful sisters of Alaska. Too soon we were on the airplane flying home.

That night I was lying in bed watching TV. My thoughts turned to the news I'd heard while in Alaska—my friend, Pat, had recently been diagnosed with breast cancer. I realized that I had gone three months without doing a breast exam. Normally, I check faithfully each month. So I checked.

And I found a lump.

*Hmmm, that's different,* I thought. I decided to go to the doctor the next day. I wasn't really worried, though. My doctor had previously commented that I had lumpy tissue. And I had absolutely no family history of cancer that I was aware of.

The next day I went to my appointment. The nurse practitioner examined me and said, "Well, it's thicker there. Let's get it checked out."

Mammogram. Ultrasound. I knew what those meant. I hadn't made it home when the doctor called. Back I went.

"Well, it doesn't look good," she said. "Let's get a biopsy."

I drove home thinking the whole way, *Wow, I could have breast cancer.*

I could barely believe what was happening.

The next few days were a blur. I flew out to speak at another Time Out for Women event. I led all the women in doing the "Dance of Joy" while thinking, *If you only knew.* I flew home and had a biopsy. I organized hundreds of volunteers for a huge Protect Marriage walk scheduled for the weekend, worked on my campaign, attended to my legal work, checked on the sisters in my ward, got my family squared away—and I flew out again for the weekend.

The next week, I was officially diagnosed with cancer. I had to fly out the next day. I couldn't tell my mom or my in-laws or anyone because I hadn't had a chance to sit down with my husband and tell my own children. I remember walking around at the Time Out for Women event in Logan, Utah, trying to cheer up. I started skipping up and down the hallway, smacking my cheeks and singing "Jesus Wants Me for a Sunbeam" so that I'd be revved up to go on stage and dance and speak of joy.

Oh, my poor heart.

The months trudged on. My own campaign was warming up. I had more tests. One evening, I attended a debate and while I was on stage, I noticed a woman in the audience wearing a wig. I realized that would be me in a few months.

Let's just say there was a lot of crying in the parking lots.

We decided not to tell anyone beyond our immediate family about my cancer. I told only the bishop and the stake presidency.

No mention was made of me stepping down from my work with the Protect Marriage Amendment. We all knew I was supposed to do the work.

Thankfully, shortly after my diagnosis, the bishop gave me a blessing, promising me that I would be completely healed. The stake president later confirmed that blessing. I came to rely heavily on that promise. I would live. I wasn't going to die.

(Now, let me pause for a brief public service announcement to all women out there and all who have women they love. *Please* do a monthly breast exam. That is what saved my life. My doctor missed it; she called the area "bumpy breast tissue"—uh, that would be a TUMOR. My mammogram missed it, though I faithfully got tested every year. I had no family history of cancer that I knew of; I had breastfed all my children. I had no risk factors other than being a woman and turning 50. You *must* check yourself regularly. You can save your own life. End of announcement.)

After the first lump was discovered, an MRI revealed a second lump. That meant more testing. More bad news. More cancer. I had to have a mastectomy.

My surgeon called. The surgery had to be done on November 4. I said we couldn't possibly do it on that day—it was election day! She asked if I was a poll worker. I broke out in rather hysterical laughter and told her that not only was I a candidate but I was also the regional coordinator for a major issue on the ballot. She told me I had no choice. We couldn't delay the surgery for even one day.

Was this some kind of cosmic joke? Of all the days of the entire year it had to be on election day?

In the middle of all of this we were also dealing with my son needing some corrective surgery. So while I was sitting down meeting my surgeon for the first time, my son was literally in surgery with his father texting me updates the whole time. Our lives were spinning out of control.

Election weekend arrived. That Saturday, we had a giant Protect Marriage rally in our community with many hundreds of volunteers. It was such a joyful day of standing for truth and righteousness. What a tremendous experience to stand shoulder to shoulder with miles of volunteers and their families.

After the rally, I went home and sent out an e-mail telling our volunteers that I would not be with them on election day. I asked them to be valiant and work hard to the end.

On election day, I went to the hospital. (Not how I pictured that day going, frankly.) I learned the cancer had spread to one lymph node and that it was not two tumors, but one large one (5.2 cm).

And it didn't stop there. I had to have a second, small surgery. Then chemotherapy. (I went bald right after Christmas. Man, that was weird.) The chemotherapy threw me into menopause a hundred miles an hour. I had constant hot flashes and absolutely no sleep. More chemotherapy. I developed bronchitis. For a month. Then I had a weird allergic reaction to some plant residue; I broke out in hives literally head to toe. For a month. Bronchitis and hives at the same time? I thought I would go insane.

I finished chemotherapy and had a couple of weeks to "recuperate" before I started my radiation treatments. That was when the stake president asked me to give a talk in stake conference. I said to him, "You do realize that I'm in the middle of all this?" He said he did. And he asked me anyway. Being able to speak about dealing with adversity while I was in the middle of dealing with adversity was a powerful experience for me.

We were hanging in there. Barely. But I guess that wasn't enough.

A couple of weeks later I was in my office and my husband was sitting on the couch. "Merrilee," he said. "I've been laid off from my job."

Shock. There is no other word for it. Complete shock to the core. It was not a complete surprise, but I had hoped and prayed that the Lord would decide we were suffering enough.

"I am going to have a hard time dealing with this," I said to my husband. I got up and went upstairs to my bed.

And proceeded to have a nearly complete emotional break-down. I began to howl. That's the only word I can use.

I howled for hours and hours. My poor husband was beside himself, pacing the room. He would alternately beg me to calm down and declare he was taking me to the hospital. But I couldn't stop. At some point, I remember my youngest son holding my hands and my husband giving me a blessing. I seem to recall that he also gave me some sleeping medication. Finally, after many hours, I fell asleep. I woke in the middle of the night and the dawning reality of our lives hit me again and I began to howl some more. More hours went by.

I have very few memories of the days that followed. I had not slept more than a few hours for months because of the chemo and menopause. I had absolutely no reserves left to be able to cope with this new trial.

I reached depths I never knew were possible. I would sit in my bed—bald, sick, and scarred. Devastated.

How would we survive? What about the health insurance? What about the mortgage? I still had to finish my cancer treat-ments. Why? Why now? Why all of this?

A few days later, I started daily radiation. And then I received news that an inactive member of our ward was dying of cancer. His wife was trying to care for him as well as her young son. She needed help. That snapped me into action. I was the Relief Society president and this family needed relief. So I would get my radiation treatment and then I'd go upstairs to the ICU to help this sweet woman care for her sick husband. And then I would go home and scramble to reduce our bills, take care of Relief Society business, and on and on. The man passed away a couple of weeks later. It was strange to arrange a funeral when you're wearing a wig and in cancer treatments yourself. It was the second funeral that year in our ward, and it was only March.

The mayor of our city was also in the same ICU dying of cancer. When he passed away a few weeks later, there was a lot of political "swirling" and speculation that I could be appointed mayor since I had been open about the fact that I had planned to run for mayor the following year.

After seven weeks of radiation treatment—and with only one more to go—I attended a city council meeting in my wig where the discussion included the possibility that I be appointed mayor. Talk about surreal. To make it worse, a young woman from my ward who had been writing letters to the newspaper editor saying that I should not be mayor because of my efforts on the Protect Marriage Amendment was at the meeting and spoke out against me. Then, a fellow council member who had been my ally for thirteen years publicly betrayed me with no warning. That was painful. I was not appointed.

At some point, my husband and I decided to sell our home and downsize both the house and the mortgage. Our youngest son was going off to college and, with my husband unemployed, it seemed like a good decision. We prayed about it and felt it was the right thing to do. So through weeks of radiation and two funerals, we were busily repairing, cleaning, and organizing our home. We held a giant garage sale to help raise money and to downsize our belongings. The house was finally ready and miracle of miracles, we found a buyer before we even listed it! Surely, the tide was finally turning!

You know how the tide goes out before a tsunami hits? It was kind of like that.

When they did the physical inspection, they discovered that the house had inexplicably settled three inches. There was no way to know when it had settled or if it had stopped. The buyers understandably fled. We now had a house we could not sell for several years.

The circumstances of our lives had profoundly changed in a year. The next night our family prayer was short. My husband prayed, "Father, please bless the food." There was a long, quiet pause. "And . . . Thy will be done." We all said amen. And all of us in unison said, "Whatever." We started to laugh. Boy, was that our lives. Whatever . . .

So I'm still in the middle of it. My husband, Steve, is still out of work. We can't sell our house. Thankfully, I've finished my treatments and I'm now on medication for five years and under close monitoring. Soon, I'll begin the first of two extensive breast reconstruction surgeries.

Yup, still in the middle. Still praying that it will slow down.

I have felt that the storms of life are beating us to a pulp. I have felt the rain, the sleet, the hurricane, and the tsunami. I feel at times like I'm just barely dog-paddling along. For several months, I was just floating on my back, trying to survive. At least I'm back to doing a little dog-paddling now.

It's been like being in a riptide, those powerful currents that run underneath the ocean. If you're in one and you try to swim directly to shore, the riptide will drag you back out to sea. As you continue to try to make forward progress, it will sap your strength. Many people have died trying to make it to the shore in a riptide. The key to surviving is to swim parallel to the beach until you find a safe area where there is no riptide.

That's pretty much where we are these days, swimming sideways and hoping that the powerful forces that are buffeting us will slow down so we can make some forward progress again. Some days we're swimming strongly, some days we're just dog-paddling along, and some days, we just float, trying to keep our heads above water. We just do what we can.

In the end, I know that my seemingly endless trials—my seemingly endless swimming—is bringing me to a place where I need to be and is making me the person I need to be.

But this book is not all about me. This book is also about you. And your own journey through trying times. When we layer on the challenges of the latter days and the difficulties facing our marriages, our children, our work, and our communities, it is likely that you, too, have a long list of trials and tribulations (which I lovingly call "TnT") that are buffeting you and weighing you down.

So what do we do? Do we curl up in bed and pull the covers over our head? Do we give up?

No!

I'm convinced that in trying times, you just keep trying!

CHAPTER 2

# Choosing to Stay True
# and Faithful

My life lately has been chaos on every level. Every part of my life—physical, spiritual, mental, emotional, financial, social, you name it—is in a state of flux. And I have often felt as though I had no choice over anything—tests, surgery, chemo, radiation, my husband losing his job, the house. For a control freak like me to have almost no control over my own life has been an unbelievable experience. One that has taught me much about the incredible power of choice.

President Henry B. Eyring, then a member of the Quorum of the Twelve, spoke of the importance of making choices even during the storms of life that beset us:

> The great test of life is to see whether we will hearken to and obey God's commands in the midst of the storms of life. It is not to endure storms, but to choose the right while they rage. And the tragedy of life is to fail in that test and so fail to qualify to return in glory to our heavenly home. . . .

Decisions now to exercise faith and be steady in obedience will in time produce great faith and assurance. That is the spiritual preparedness we all will need. And it will qualify us in the moments of crisis to receive the Lord's promise that "if ye are prepared ye shall not fear."

That will be true when we face the storms of life and the prospect of death. A loving Heavenly Father and His Beloved Son have given us all the help They can to pass the test of life set before us. But we must decide to obey and then do it. We build the faith to pass the tests of obedience over time and through our daily choices. We can decide now to do quickly whatever God asks of us. And we can decide to be steady in the small tests of obedience which build the faith to carry us through the great tests, which will surely come.[1]

We know this life is a test, right? We will be tried and tested and proven. But wherever we are in our trials—whether at the beginning, stuck in the middle, or nearing what we hope will be the end, we can take heart that we still have choices—important choices—that can and will directly affect the outcome of our trials.

## The Test of Abraham

I've been thinking about Abraham a lot. I've also been thinking about Sarah. As I've been going through everything, a few people have asked me, "Do you think this is your Abrahamic test?" I've been wondering.

Abraham's test is, of course, the classic extreme test of faithfulness.

> And it came to pass after these things, that God did tempt [Hebrew: test, or prove] Abraham, and said unto him, Abraham: and he said, Behold, here I am.

13

And he said, Take now thy son, thine only son Isaac, whom thou lovest, and get thee into the land of Moriah; and offer him there for a burnt offering upon one of the mountains which I will tell thee of.

And Abraham rose up early in the morning, and saddled his ass, and took two of his young men with him, and Isaac his son, and clave the wood for the burnt offering, and rose up, and went unto the place of which God had told him. . . .

And Abraham took the wood of the burnt offering, and laid it upon Isaac his son; and he took the fire in his hand, and a knife; and they went both of them together.

And Isaac spake unto Abraham his father, and said, My father: and he said, Here am I, my son. And he said, Behold the fire and the wood: but where is the lamb for a burnt offering?

And Abraham said, My son, God will provide himself a lamb for a burnt offering: so they went both of them together.

And they came to the place which God had told him of; and Abraham built an altar there, and laid the wood in order, and bound Isaac his son, and laid him on the altar upon the wood.

And Abraham stretched forth his hand, and took the knife to slay his son.

And the angel of the Lord called unto him out of heaven, and said, Abraham, Abraham: and he said, Here am I.

And he said, Lay not thine hand upon the lad, neither do thou any thing unto him: for now I know that thou fearest God, seeing thou hast not withheld thy son, thine only son from me. (Genesis 22:1–3, 6–12)

I cannot imagine how difficult this test must have been for Abraham. And I have wondered if this test also involved Sarah. Did she know? I don't know. But she certainly was tested and tried by her experience of a lifetime of barrenness before being blessed with a child.

As I have pondered Abraham's experience, I have realized something. What was the purpose of this test? Did Heavenly Father or Jehovah *not* know what would happen? Of course not. They weren't surprised. They absolutely knew what Abraham and his family would do.

So what was the purpose? I suspect that part of the purpose of this test was to prove to *Abraham* himself what he would do. In that moment, he learned he would be faithful—no matter what. He learned he was strong enough to do the will of the Lord—no matter what. Not only did Abraham prove to the Lord that "thou fearest God" (Genesis 22:12) but he also proved to himself that his faithfulness was true and abiding at a very, very deep level.

I believe that the difficulties and tests we are given in life are given to us in large part to teach *us* strength and confidence. We learn whether or not we will be true and faithful. The Lord explains this process in Doctrine and Covenants 101:4–5: "Therefore, they must needs be chastened and tried, even as Abraham, who was commanded to offer up his only son. For all those who will not endure chastening, but deny me, cannot be sanctified."

That's a critical question. Will we go through our trials and not deny the Lord? Will we, like Abraham, make the right choice?

One thing is clear. It is in those moments of testing and trial that we make the choice to stay strong and faithful—no matter what.

## Keeping Perspective

So many of us are facing difficulties right now. Each of us has spent many days and nights wondering if the darkness will ever pass. We are facing a fearful and unknown future. And latter-day events are hitting faster and faster. Elder Neal A. Maxwell commented on these days.

> We cannot expect to live in a time when men's hearts will fail them except the faithful experience a few fibrillations themselves. We won't be entirely immune from feelings that go with these fibrillations.
>
> Though our view of eternity is reasonably clear, it is often our view of the next mile which may be obscured! Hence the need for the constancy of the gift of the Holy Ghost. I think you will see this a number of times in your lives. You have cast your minds forward and are fixed on the things of eternity, and all of that is proper and good, but there is sometimes fog in the next hundred yards. You can make it through, but don't be surprised when it is the short-term obscurity through which you must pass as a result of your faith in the long-term things.
>
> How can we expect to overcome the world if we are too insulated from its trials and challenges? You will experience at times what might be called some redemptive turbulence. Think, for instance, of the Master and the roiling Sea of Galilee, tossed by the "wind boisterous" and "contrary," and the anguished cry of His followers as in the lyrics we sing, "Master, the tempest is raging." Yet that tempest actually occurred on a tiny little sea only 12 miles by 7 miles! Nevertheless, for that moment, Galilee constituted the real world for those anxious disciples![2]

I don't know about you, but I'm certainly experiencing fibrillations—indeed, I'd say I've been having some full-blown attacks!

But that perspective—that for the disciples, the small area of

Galilee was the whole world to them—applies to each of us. Our individual and personal challenges loom large and consume our attention and our lives while we are going through them. Yet, it's important that we keep some long-term perspective.

On the one hand, you may think, "Oh, man, my life is so much more difficult than his (or hers)!" It's an ironic fact that we can experience pride even when comparing our trials and tribulations! I've done it though; when I encounter women who had a lumpectomy, I think, "Oh, that would have been so much easier!" It is tempting to be competitive even in the midst of our tests.

On the other hand, you may be told of someone with truly egregious trials, and you may think, "Well, at least I don't have it that bad. I shouldn't complain." But that viewpoint isn't right either.

It is useless to compare our trials with others. For each of us, the things we are facing right now are real and significant. Comparing them to others neither makes our trials bigger nor smaller than they really are. Each of us has our own customized testing plan, designed to prove us and reveal to us what we're made of.

## Submission Can Lead to Strength

We believe in a Heavenly Father who is both aware of and in control of our lives. When our lives spin out of control, we may be tempted to resist these events, question God, and wonder if He loves us at all.

It's normal to wonder "Why?" Why did you lose your job? Why did your wife leave you? Why did the accident happen? Why did he get sick? Why? Why? Why?

And at the root of all those questions is the big one: "Why did God let this happen?"

Frankly, we may never know the answer to that question. But I do know this. I *know* that God loves you and He loves me. Of that I have no doubt. And I know that *love* is at the base of all that He has planned for our lives.

Knowing that, then, leaves us with a choice. We can choose to submit to His will willingly . . . or not.

Elder Neal A. Maxwell said it so eloquently:

> The submission of one's will is really the only uniquely personal thing we have to place on God's altar. The many other things we "give" . . . are actually the things He has already given or loaned us. However, when you and I finally submit ourselves, by letting our individual wills be swallowed up in God's will, then we are really giving something to Him! It is the only possession which is truly ours to give![3]

Of course the best choice for us is to choose to submit to God's will *willingly.* This may seem the antithesis of choosing to be strong, but actually, it is the beginning of true strength.

When I think of submissive strength, I think of Mary, the mother of Jesus. There she was, living her life. She must have been so happy—engaged to the wonderful Joseph. And he was truly wonderful. After all, he was chosen to be the earthly father of the Messiah. And then in a moment, her life radically changed. She was called upon to do the greatest thing that had ever been asked of a woman. It was incredible. But it was also a dramatic shift in what she had planned for her life. I can only imagine the thoughts that were racing through her head as she contemplated her future.

And she chose strength.

The angel said to her, "For with God nothing shall be impossible" (Luke 1:37), simultaneously reassuring and explaining to Mary what was to be. And Mary responded with positive strength, "Behold the handmaid of the Lord; be it unto me according to thy word" (Luke 1:38). Sometimes I think we read those words with a passive resignation that her life is changed and she'll go along with it. But as I've pondered this statement, I like to read it with strength of conviction. With boldness: **"Behold the handmaid of the Lord; be it unto me according to thy word."**

Mary willingly chose submission to the will of the Lord. She chose strength. As time progressed, she gained even more strength and understanding. The scriptures recount, "And Mary said, My soul doth magnify the Lord, and my spirit hath rejoiced in God my Saviour. For he hath regarded the low estate of his handmaiden: for, behold, from henceforth all generations shall call me blessed" (Luke 1:46–48). After pondering the enormous change in her life and the greatness of the task placed before her, she realized that she would be incredibly blessed for all eternity. Her willing submission had led her to greater strength.

The Lord doesn't want passive submission. He wants active, willing submission where we move toward strength and understanding. The Prophet Joseph Smith, shortly after he had been allowed to escape his captors in Missouri, reflected on his feelings,

> During the time I was in the hands of my enemies, I must say, that although I felt great anxiety respecting my family and friends, who were so inhumanly treated and abused, . . . yet as far as I was concerned, I felt perfectly calm, and *resigned to the will of my Heavenly Father.*[4]

I read that quote during Relief Society and the phrase "resigned to the will of my Heavenly Father" resonated with me. I understood how Joseph could at once make that declaration of submission and yet also state that he felt perfectly calm about the entire matter. He was willing to let the Father control his life in every particular.

## Timing Is Everything

But even as we submit to the will of the Lord, sometimes we have questions about the timing. This was a huge question for me. I understood the "why" of the whole cancer thing, but I sure didn't understand the timing. I didn't spend a whole lot of time asking, "Why me?"—mainly because I figured the answer to that question was "Why *not* me?"—but I sure did ask, "Why *now?*"

I kept thinking, "Two months. I just needed two more months!" In two months, both campaigns would have been finished and my speaking tour wrapped up. Two measly months! Couldn't cancer have waited? I would ask that question rather rhetorically in my constant prayers, but still hoping to gain an answer. I did receive an answer, but not until many months had gone by. As I struggled with the question of timing, I remembered the many comments Elder Neal A. Maxwell had made on the topic, including this one:

> Others have a generalized faith in God's overall purposes but are frustrated and irritated with its tactical dimensions, such as God's particularized timing as especially applied to them. But how can we question God's timing without questioning His omniscience?[5]

"Frustrated" and "irritated" pretty well summed up how I was feeling. I knew that I may never have my question of "Why now?"

answered in this lifetime, but I knew that I did believe in His omniscience. I did not doubt that there was a divine purpose to the timing. And, whether or not I understood it, I knew it would be a blessing to me.

President Dieter F. Uchtdorf described it perfectly,

> The answers to our prayers come in the Lord's due time. Sometimes we may become frustrated that the Lord has delayed answering our prayers. In such times we need to understand that He knows what we do not know. He sees what we do not see. Trust in Him. He knows what is best for His child, and being a perfect God, He will answer our prayers perfectly and in the perfect time.[6]

In the perfect time. I had to accept that I needed to let go of that question. Knowing the answer would not have changed the reality of the situation. It is the same for all of us. We must trust in God's perfect timing. And we must also realize that part of our test of faith is to also have faith in His timing as well.

## Suffering Can Be a Gift

It seems that the country (maybe the entire world) is in a period of great suffering—the kind of turmoil we have not seen in many decades. Unemployment, economic loss, war, and political and moral conflict besiege us on all sides. Virtually no one is immune.

The state of suffering has been a recurring theme in the past few general conferences. President Thomas S. Monson said this,

> Since last we met together in a general conference six months ago, there have been continuing signs that circumstances in the world aren't necessarily as we would wish. The

global economy, which six months ago appeared to be sagging, seems to have taken a nosedive, and for many weeks now the financial outlook has been somewhat grim. In addition, the moral footings of society continue to slip, while those who attempt to safeguard those footings are often ridiculed and, at times, picketed and persecuted. Wars, natural disasters, and personal misfortunes continue to occur.

It would be easy to become discouraged and cynical about the future—or even fearful of what might come—if we allowed ourselves to dwell only on that which is wrong in the world and in our lives.[7]

Indeed. I had almost stopped watching the news completely because it was so depressing and my desire to deal with the world at large was overly taxed. We are all facing trauma on a scale that has not been seen in a long time.

But whether our trials are large or small, we can take comfort in knowing that we are not alone. Elder Jeffrey R. Holland related,

We are not alone. . . . When suffering, we may in fact be nearer to God than we've ever been in our entire lives. *That* knowledge can turn every situation into a would-be temple. . . . And it certainly underscores the fact that the righteous— in the Savior's case, the personification of righteousness—can be totally worthy before God and still suffer.[8]

I think we sometimes tell ourselves that if we live a righteous life, if we are completely true and faithful, that nothing bad or hard will ever happen to us. That is not true.

But it is a common reaction. If something bad happens, we immediately evaluate our spirituality to see if somehow we have brought this affliction upon ourselves. To be honest, sometimes we are sinning and that can bring difficult things into our lives. But more often than not, trials just come as part of our life experience.

Every single person in the world is probably having a trial right now. And if not, they probably will be by the end of the day! Hard things happen.

Elder Neal A. Maxwell wrote,

> Inwardly and anxiously we may worry, too, that an omniscient and loving God sees more stretch in us than we feel we have. Hence when God is actually lifting us up, we may feel He is letting us down.[9]

I am convinced that suffering should not be an unwelcome thing. Sometimes it's the best way to teach us the things we need to learn and help us to become who we need to be.

When I was diagnosed with cancer, I spent some time pondering the significance of this event in my life. Certainly, it was a difficult burden to face. And the difficulty was made infinitely greater because I was already in the middle of dealing with many other difficult burdens.

I wasn't looking forward to the suffering that I would have to go through. I knew I would suffer great physical pain and sickness. I knew I would also suffer a drastic change in my appearance that would be difficult to cope with. And I knew my family would suffer. It was natural to wonder about the purpose of it all.

I was blessed to know almost immediately that this was the Lord's will in my life. I knew that He had allowed this experience to come into my life for a very specific reason. I knew there were certain things I needed to learn that I could learn in no other way. Looking back over the last year, I can see that this is true. There have been many things I have learned that I would not have learned without these experiences.

I also knew these things were being given to me to help me become who I need to be. There was no other way.

As I have experienced tremendous and ongoing suffering, I have drawn closer to my Lord. I have spent many hours contemplating His suffering. And I have come to two conclusions:

Suffering should not be an unwelcome thing.

Suffering can be a great gift.

So we must put aside feelings that trials are a punishment in our lives. Often the opposite is true. And let us never forget that Christ lived a *perfect* life and yet He suffered more than all of us combined. Indeed, He took upon Himself all of our suffering in His consuming love for each of us.

## Bearing Our Burdens

Many times we quote the part of 1 Corinthians 10:13 that says God will never give us more than we can bear. Yet there is more to that scripture that we often overlook: "There hath no temptation taken you but such as is common to man: but God is faithful, who will not suffer you to be tempted [or tried] above that ye are able; *but will with the temptation also make a way to escape, that ye may be able to bear it*" (1 Corinthians 10:13; emphasis added).

I believe that God *will* allow us to have more than we can bear because it is often only when we are pushed to our limits—or beyond—that we surrender ourselves to God. It is in that moment that He can truly help us. And, as the scripture promises, He has planned a way for our escape, a way for us to bear our burdens.

Early in my trials, the Spirit prompted me to read some scriptures that have come to hold great meaning to me. In the Book of Mormon, the story is told of Alma and his people who have been converted but are in bondage to the Lamanites. They were severely punished for praying vocally to God for help.

> And Alma and his people did not raise their voices to the Lord their God, but did pour out their hearts to him; and he did know the thoughts of their hearts.
>
> And it came to pass that the voice of the Lord came to them in their afflictions, saying: Lift up your heads and be of good comfort, for I know of the covenant which ye have made unto me; and I will covenant with my people and deliver them out of bondage.
>
> And I will also *ease the burdens* which are put upon your shoulders, that even you cannot feel them upon your backs, even while you are in bondage; and this will I do that ye may stand as witnesses for me hereafter, and that ye may know of a surety that I, the Lord God, do visit my people in their afflictions. (Mosiah 24:12–14; emphasis added)

He may not remove our burdens. But he *will* make them bearable. Those verses came to me over and over again throughout the last year. And I can testify that the Lord God does visit His people in their afflictions. I know because He has visited me.

I remember the day of my bone scan clearly. I had to have a scan to determine if the cancer had spread, and in my research on the procedure, I learned that cancer shows up as a bright spot on the scan.

Well, I waited nervously for the injection—you know it's not a great idea when the doctor comes in with the syringe in a little, lead-lined box!

The whole time the scan was taking place, a song kept buzzing in my head. The words came first, and it took a while for me to figure out what it was. It was the second verse to "We Thank Thee, O God, for a Prophet":

> *When dark clouds of trouble hang o'er us*
> *And threaten our peace to destroy,*
> *There is hope smiling brightly before us,*
> *And we know that deliv'rance is nigh.*
> *We doubt not the Lord nor his goodness.*
> *We've proved him in days that are past.*
> *The wicked who fight against Zion*
> *Will surely be smitten at last.*[10]

I kept clinging to the words of that hymn. I did not doubt the Lord. I knew that He would extend goodness to me.

Soon the scan was done, and I got up to collect my wallet and keys and happened to glance at the screen. My cancer was in my left breast and there on my left shoulder was a bright spot with a smaller bright spot on my right shoulder. I was shocked. It looked like my cancer had spread to my bones.

Needless to say, the drive home was stressful. I was so worried that the cancer had spread and that the treatments I would be facing would be significantly increased.

My husband and I pulled up to the front of the house and I noticed there were boxes and boxes on the porch. About thirty thousand literature pieces for the Protect Marriage Amendment had arrived and had to be distributed by the end of the day to the various volunteers.

I stood there on the porch for a moment. Then I told my

husband, "I cannot handle this." I went upstairs to my room and collapsed on my bed and eventually fell into a fitful sleep.

My dear husband worked quickly sorting the materials and getting the volunteers lined up to collect them. When I woke, I helped him finish up the work.

I realized something that day. There were many things that I was encountering (and would continue to encounter) that were more than I could bear. I cannot tell you the number of times I turned to my Heavenly Father and flat out said, "I cannot handle this." But every time I reached that breaking point, the Lord was right there, ready to help.

He never gives us anything that we can't handle *with His help*.

(And, luckily, my cancer had not spread to my bones after all. That was a treasured blessing.)

## A Personal Test; a Personal Choice

My God is a personal God. He is personal to me. He is with me always. He is there in every moment for me. And His love is there in every moment for me.

And for you. You, too, are His child, and you, too, have His complete attention. Incredible, isn't it? In times of pain and suffering, He is right there for you. In all times, He is with you.

Elder Jeffrey R. Holland wrote,

> There are plenty of troubles in the world, but there have always been troubles in every age and era. Don't be preoccupied with them and don't be discouraged by them. Our time is filled with wonderful opportunities and great blessings.[11]

As we face trying times in our lives, we need to realize that within them are found great opportunities for growth that we could experience in no other way. Each of us is being blessed right now with many trials of all shapes, sizes, and descriptions. They are unique to each of us and to this time in our lives.

Each of our trials and experiences will show us what we're made of. Each of us will have or are currently experiencing an Abrahamic test of our own. Each of us will face that day and that time when we plumb the depths of our soul, and in our anguish, make a choice. The choice we make to stay strong and faithful will reveal to us who we are. We will find out what we're made of.

# CHAPTER 3

# Choosing to Be Positive and Grateful

As my trials mounted and as I felt more and more out of control, I realized that I had control over one primary choice—my attitude. Despite what was going on around me, I could control my own head—my own will. Some days it felt like that was pretty much all I could control.

When faced with challenges, each of us has a choice presented to us. What will we chose?

We can choose whether we will be weak or strong. It's interesting to ponder that choice. I think it takes a lot of emotional energy to be weak. To be miserable and sad and depressed and discouraged and fearful takes a lot of work! Think of all the emotional energy that goes into those choices. It's pretty significant. Now consider how much emotional energy it takes to be strong. It takes effort to be strong and courageous and positive and brave, but I would contend that it takes less energy than choosing to be weak.

I knew I wanted to choose to be strong, but my choice was tested on a daily and sometimes hourly basis. I knew it was the right choice and the best choice for me but it was certainly not an easy one.

I have come to look upon trials and tribulations for what they really are: strengthening opportunities. Doesn't that change how they feel? Our challenges are tremendous opportunities to choose strength and to grow stronger as we do so.

So as we experience these "strengthening opportunities," what attitude should we choose?

## Be of Good Cheer

A few days after I found my lump and was facing an unknown future, my bishop gave me a blessing. He sat and chatted with me and my husband and then began my blessing. He spoke generally for a while, but then he paused and began to speak to me very directly. My journal records what he said,

> Then he blessed me so directly, "Be of good cheer. You will be able to handle this. Be of good cheer." He asked that God would bless me with physical strength to bear what I needed to and with spiritual strength to know that Heavenly Father was wrapping me in His arms of love. Oh, I loved that because that is EXACTLY how I feel. . . . Then he paused and blessed me that I would be healed through my faith—completely healed through my faith—and that all would be well. That I would have the support of all those around me—my husband, my sons, my sisters, and everyone else who loved me. And he repeated that I would be HEALED and all would be well and that my body would be returned to strong health and vigor.

He said that I would be able to handle all the many responsibilities that the Lord had assigned to me.

At the time, I thought it was rather strange that my bishop was counseling me to be of good cheer. I like to think that I have, to quote Joseph Smith, a "native cheery temperament" (Joseph Smith–History 1:28). I had no idea how much my optimism would be tested.

A week later I was sitting in stake conference and I heard the whisperings of the Spirit asking if I wanted to know the results of the biopsy. It took me about half the meeting to find my courage, but I finally answered that, yes, I did want to know. And in great clarity, I knew. I did indeed have breast cancer. After the meeting, and in the safety of the beloved parking lot, I told my husband what I had felt and what I had come to know. Later that night, I called the bishop.

"Bishop, I just want to let you know that I do have cancer."

"Did you get the biopsy results?"

"No," I replied.

"Well, let's just be positive," he replied.

"OK, Bishop, I'm *positive* that I have breast cancer!"

I think that was staying positive, don't you?

Joseph Smith faced the same choice to stay positive. He stated, "Yes, that still small voice, which has so often whispered consolation to my soul, in the depths of sorrow and distress, bade me be of good cheer, and promised deliverance, which gave me great comfort."[1]

And in his time of darkest trial, he wrote, "Let us cheerfully do all things that lie in our power; and then may we stand still, with the utmost assurance, to see the salvation of God, and for his arm to be revealed" (D&C 123:17).

The Lord also has encouraged us to be of good cheer: "Wherefore, be of good cheer, and do not fear, for I the Lord am with you, and will stand by you; and ye shall bear record of me, even Jesus Christ, that I am the Son of the living God, that I was, that I am, and that I am to come" (D&C 68:6).

Be of good cheer. Don't worry, be happy.

Easier said than done.

I like to take a long walk each morning and pray—it's a transforming experience for me—and even on the darkest days, I would make myself smile and say, "I am cheerful! I am happy! I am choosing to be positive!" Some days I said it through tears and pain. Many days. But each day I tried to choose to be cheerful and that simple choice made an amazing difference.

One Sunday I was at church, conducting Relief Society. I was sporting an especially stylish cream-colored hat and looking pretty snappy, even if I was in a fog of chemo. After the lesson, a woman came up to me and said, "Sister, I want to see your hair under your hat!"

I replied, "Oh, sister, I don't have any hair. I'm bald."

She seemed rather confused by that for a moment, even though I had told her I was in chemo. "No, I want to see under your hat!"

I kept smiling. "Uh, sister, there's nothing under there."

But she was insistent and asked a third time.

So I lifted up my hat, and she gasped. "Sister! You as bald as a baby's bottom!"

I chuckled and said, "Yup, that's the truth."

She peered into my eyes and asked me, "But how can you be so happy and positive? You have no hair and you are sick. How can you be smiling?"

It was a moment when time stood still. I looked back into her eyes and said, "It's just hair. It will grow back. Every day I am faced with a choice. I can choose to be miserable and depressed or I can choose to be cheerful and positive. I choose to be positive."

I can testify of the power of that choice. And when I was going through major chemical treatments, that choice was physically lifesaving. I would bound into my chemo treatments sporting my colorful "Survivor" buff of the week, the TV show's logo blazoned on the front. I would smile and laugh and chat with the other patients as we all sat hooked up to our IV's that were dripping liquid poisons into us. Bringing a positive attitude with me to my treatments made all the difference. Those who were negative and complained seemed to be suffering more than those who were willing to smile. I was grateful for the words of a bishop who had no idea that his counsel would literally make a significant difference in how my body responded to what I was dealing with.

We can choose to be of good cheer. It is a monumental choice.

Now many a time, I was not so cheery. Oh, yeah. You cannot go through everything that we are all going through and be a perky "Pollyanna" the entire time. But I tried to view my challenges like getting tipped over in a canoe. You have to immediately get to work turning it over, and even if it's filled with water, you're in a more stable and safe position.

As I've navigated this past year, I've noticed a difference in those who choose to be cheerful. There are the grumpy unemployed, and there are the hopeful unemployed. There are the depressed sick, and there are the patient sick (get it?). There are those who are discouraged in heavy callings, and there are those who are valiant in heavy callings. Night and day difference between each.

We have enough burdens in life to carry around. It seems silly to add in heavy rocks labeled "fear," "sadness," and "discouragement." Those are heavy, heavy rocks indeed. Instead, as we choose cheer, I like to visualize sturdy, helium-filled balloons tied to our burdens, helping to lift the load.

Sometimes choosing to be cheerful takes a little bit of creativity and effort! I was recuperating from surgery and in a lot of pain but still trying to be cheerful. My bishop sent me one of those musical cards with James Brown singing, "Oh, I feel good! I knew that I would!" When I opened it up the first time, I almost laughed myself off my bed. Every morning after that, I would get out of bed and open that card and sing at the top of my lungs, "Oh, I feel good! I knew that I would!" My husband always knew when I was awake and functioning each morning because he'd hear me singing. I played that card every day until it finally broke. Such a simple thing, but a daily choice of cheerfulness! And you know what? I felt a whole lot better. No matter what my body was telling me, I was singing!

Our ward Christmas party happened to fall in the middle of my chemo treatments. I sat at a table next to my friend who had been in charge of the event and who had spent part of that day in the emergency room with a health issue of her own. Before the party got started, the brother giving the opening prayer paused and with great feeling asked the Lord to bless all those who were sick or afflicted. I began to giggle. After the prayer, I tapped my friend on the shoulder. "Hey, Jill. You're sick and I'm afflicted!" We laughed together. We also started a new club—the "I'm Sick of Being Afflicted" club.

I am convinced that choosing to be cheerful is one of the most powerful choices of attitude we can make. No matter what hits, we can choose a positive attitude and that choice will make a huge difference in our ability to endure and cope.

## Turn to God

Another part of our choice of attitude has to do with our choices relative to God. What will our attitude be toward the Lord Himself? Like Abraham, we have a choice to make. Will we deny God? Or will we submit to His will? What will we choose?

Many years ago, I was in the process of doing an estate plan for my piano tuner. He was a young man, married, and with a young child. When I didn't hear from him for several weeks, I called. He answered and with great anguish in his voice, he told me that his wife had died suddenly. She was only twenty-eight years old and in perfect health. He recounted how she had grabbed her head and literally dropped dead in front of him and their child.

And then he broke down. "My daughter asked why this happened to her mother. She asked how could God do this to us. I told her that God doesn't love us."

I tried to reassure him that God *did* love him, but he was not to be comforted. I watched him over the next several years become bitter, angry, and resentful. His faith and the faith of his child was destroyed in the process. It was an extraordinarily painful thing to watch him reject God and lose the peace he so desperately sought.

I remember facing the same choice either to turn to God or to turn away. It was 1994. My husband was out of work and it looked like it would be a long time before things would turn around due to the state of the economy. I can remember so clearly sitting outside on a clear night and talking with my husband about the difficult circumstances we were in. And I discussed this choice that we had to make.

"Honey, we can choose to get really bitter, angry, or resentful against God. If we do, it will destroy our faith and it will destroy our kids. Or we can choose to react with faith, patience, love, and gratitude. If we do that, it will deepen our children's faith and testimonies and our own."

It turned out to be an easy choice after all.

Now, as we look back on that very long year so long ago, we see how the seeds of deep testimony were planted for each of our children. They gained incredible testimonies of prayer, fasting, faith, and obedience which bless them to this day.

The choice of our attitude toward God can either open or close the door to receiving help. Elder Jeffrey R. Holland said,

> Remaining true to our Christian principles is the only way divine influence can help us. The Spirit has a near-impossible task to get through to a heart that is filled with hate or anger or vengeance or *self-pity.* Those are all antithetical to the Spirit of the Lord. On the other hand, the Spirit finds instant access to a heart striving to be charitable and forgiving, long-suffering and kind—principles of true discipleship.[2]

The choice seems simple and yet it is pivotal. Either we love the Father, or we don't. Either we trust Him, or we don't. Either we have faith in our Savior and His Atonement, or we don't. We cannot have it both ways.

But if we do . . . oh, if we do, then we have access to love and care and help that is unfathomable.

Will we take our pain and our fear and our suffering and turn to Him? We can carry our heavy burdens and lay them at His feet. We can bring our tears and our worries and turn to Him, the One who desires to succor us and gather us in His arms "as a hen gathereth her chickens" (D&C 10:65; 29:2).

I can testify that in the very moment we turn to Him, He is there! Every single time I would cry out to Him, even in the dark hours of the night, I would hear immediately, "Merrilee, I am right here." I would instantly feel His love and caring concern.

He is there for you as well. I understand that you may be suffering so greatly that it is difficult for you to feel His love. But please know that He is right there. He has never left you for a moment.

# Be Grateful

As we choose to turn to God, we can choose not only to live in the presence of love, but we can choose to be grateful as well. Such great strength emanates from that choice.

I remember being in the MRI machine. (It is *so* not like on TV! On TV, it's this quiet, calm machine just chugging out cool images. I knew I was in for a very different experience when the technician handed me earplugs.) The machine takes images very, very slowly so you have to remain perfectly still for a very, very long time. All the while the machine is clanging and banging away. I had made a conscious choice that I would go through everything in my "Trials and Tribulations Lab Experiment" with gratitude. That day was no different. Rather than focus on the pain or the claustrophobia I felt, I decided to be thankful. I began to sing one of my favorite Primary songs, "I Am Glad for Many Things," accompanied by the odd, banging noises of the MRI machine.

On another day I was lying under the radiation machine. What an amazing piece of technology! It is so precise that they have a physicist who makes the exact calculations to pinpoint which important areas to radiate and which areas to protect. This giant machine was above me, shining a red grid of light on my chest. I looked up at that incredible invention that was saving my life and began to pray. I prayed a prayer of gratitude for the inventors of that technology. I prayed over the inventors of the software that ran the machine in such a precise way. I was grateful for the radiologist (such a dear, kind man) and for all the technicians (so kind and so competent). I was thankful for all the thousands of women and men who had gone before me and who had bravely endured treatments and medical trials so that the doctors would gain knowledge. Every day that I had to lay under that machine, I prayed prayers of gratitude.

What a source of strength a grateful attitude can be! And I have seen it working in the lives of others. Recently, we were organizing a local service project to collect cleaning supplies for unemployed families. A woman who had just been through an extremely painful divorce contacted me. She had very little money, but she had been saving a little bit each month in her "service fund." She said, "I am so grateful for all the help I have received from so many people. I just want to give back to express that gratitude." Off she went to the store with her "service" money to buy cleaning supplies for other families who were suffering and in need.

The principle of gratitude can become the foundation of our strength. That choice, made regularly, completely changes the way in which we pass through the trying times that beset us. It doesn't take much. Each day can be filled with tiny little prayers of gratitude. I'm thankful I have a little bit of hair on my head! Sheena is thankful she has a part-time job cleaning homes. Doug is thankful he can walk up the street. Phil is thankful his car started this morning. And Marybeth is thankful that it is a beautiful day. Small, simple prayers to express gratitude for small, simple blessings. And "by small and simple things are great things brought to pass" (Alma 37:6).

We can choose our attitude. We can choose what we will do with our agency and will.

We can choose strength. We can choose to be of good cheer and to focus on the positive in our lives. We can choose to willingly submit to the will of the Lord in our lives and have confidence in His will and His timing. We can choose to have an attitude of love and faith in the Lord. And finally, we can choose to live our lives with a foundation of gratitude.

Each of these choices is ours alone. No one can make them for us. No one can force us to choose one way or the other. But I testify that as we make these good choices, love and blessings will flow into our lives. We will have the Spirit as our companion. And we will have peace. Truly, in the midst of serious afflictions, it is the only way we will have peace.

CHAPTER 4

# Choosing to Learn and Grow

Many years ago, I was teaching Sunday School and I asked the class to raise their hands if they had experienced a major adversity in their lives. Almost every hand went up. Then I asked, "How many of you would give up that experience?" All the same hands went back up—with enthusiasm. Oops! I realized I had asked the wrong question! "How many of you would give up all the *learning* that you gained from that experience?" The hands all went back down.

None of us is thrilled over experiencing trying times. I doubt any of us have prayed to request trials and tribulations to come into our lives. But when they do come, they invariably bring blessings with them if we will let them.

In the crowning explanation of the role of adversity in our lives, the Lord states:

> If thou art called to pass through tribulation; if thou art in

perils among false brethren; if thou art in perils among rob-
bers; if thou art in perils by land or by sea;

If thou art accused with all manner of false accusations; if
thine enemies fall upon thee; if they tear thee from the society
of thy father and mother and brethren and sisters; and if with
a drawn sword thine enemies tear thee from the bosom of thy
wife, and of thine offspring, and thine elder son, although but
six years of age, shall cling to thy garments, and shall say, My
father, my father, why can't you stay with us? O, my father,
what are the men going to do with you? and if then he shall be
thrust from thee by the sword, and thou be dragged to prison,
and thine enemies prowl around thee like wolves for the blood
of the lamb;

And if thou shouldst be cast into the pit, or into the hands
of murderers, and the sentence of death passed upon thee; if
thou be cast into the deep; if the billowing surge conspire
against thee; if fierce winds become thine enemy; if the heav-
ens gather blackness, and all the elements combine to hedge
up the way; and above all, if the very jaws of hell shall gape
open the mouth wide after thee, know thou, my son, that *all
these things shall give thee experience, and shall be for thy good.*
(D&C 122:5–7; emphasis added)

We could add if you're unemployed, if your business folded,
if your life savings have dwindled through no fault of your own,
if your marriage is suffering, if your kids are wayward, if your
health is poor, if, if, if . . .

Experience is good. There are blessings awaiting us when we
are "called" to pass through tribulation.

Certainly we can endure trying times and not gain the bene-
fit or understanding that is available to us. To obtain the full
"good" from the experience requires a choice on our part. We must

choose to approach these strengthening opportunities with an open mind looking for learning.

Even though we're still in the middle of our "strengthening opportunity," I can honestly say that I would never trade what I have learned from these experiences. Never.

I love this quote by Ronald E. Osborn: "Undertake something that is difficult; it will do you good. Unless you try to do something beyond what you have already mastered, you will never grow."[1]

From the beginning of my difficult trials, I was blessed with an assurance that I was being given these experiences to be able to learn things that I could learn in no other way. I would often encounter people who would say, "Oh, you poor thing! This is so awful!" or "Man, you guys have sure had it rough." Each time, I would brightly respond, "This is a great opportunity! We are learning so much!"

In fact, as I encountered others who were suffering in similar ways, I would ask, "So, how is your learning experience going?" It was fun to see them step back, reflect, and respond, "You're right! I'm learning a ton!" It's true. These strengthening experiences provide some of the best, most intense, and deepest learning we may ever experience.

When President Henry B. Eyring was a member of the Quorum of the Twelve, he observed,

> Your life is carefully watched over. . . . The Lord knows both what He will need you to do and what you will need to know. He is kind and He is all-knowing. So you can with confidence expect that He has prepared opportunities for you to learn in preparation for the service you will give. You will not recognize those opportunities perfectly. . . . But when you put the spiritual things first in your life, you will be blessed to feel

directed toward certain learning, and you will be motivated to work harder.[2]

I know that a lot of those learning opportunities are to be found in trying times and that a big part of those experiences is to prepare us for the future path of our lives.

Ponder for a moment a time when you went through a challenge or trial in your life. What did you learn from that experience? I began to make a list of the things I've learned from this past year and it was an eye-opening, incredible exercise! Lessons learned included:

| | |
|:---:|:---:|
| Humility | Physical strength |
| Patience with self, others, and God | Confidence |
| Empathy | Priesthood |
| Priorities | The ability to say "no"! |
| Perspective | Desire for growth |
| Love | Charity |
| Gratitude | Prudence |
| Faith | Spiritual gifts |
| Hope | Dependence on God |
| Repentance | Provident Living |
| Prayer | Self-control |
| Fasting | Forgiveness |

And that is only part of the list! The learning has gone on and on and on.

It is astounding to contemplate the amount and level of learning from just one trial or one experience. What a gift!

## Learning to Ask

Choosing to ask the question, "What am I to learn from this experience?" can be a powerful way to open the door to gaining understanding and being receptive to the teachings of the Spirit. Asking that question can take a difficult experience and turn it into a growing experience. But it can be a hard question to ask when we are in the middle of a trial. So how can we choose to learn and grow?

First, stay open to the lessons that will come your way. Sometimes, out of fear or fatigue—or both—we shut down our mind and heart, making it hard for us to grow. It may sound strange, but I think it helps to physically visualize our mind being open to the learning that is out there for us. It would be easy to wall up our hearts, especially when they are hurting so much. It takes great courage to open our hearts precisely *when* we are hurting. If we're able to do that, amazing things can happen. Said another way, when we keep our hearts and mind softened and humble and willing, we are more receptive to the lessons that have been prepared for us.

Second, pray for learning. I knew our experiences were specifically designed for us to learn certain things. I just had no clue what they were! And frankly, I didn't want to go through all of the pain, suffering, and agony and *not* learn something that was important! So I prayed. Always. Constantly. I prayed and prayed.

My constant, fervent prayer was that I would learn what I was supposed to learn and that the messages I needed to hear would pierce the haze. I remember telling the Lord many times that I was pretty foggy from chemo and from plain old sadness. I asked Him to use other people to teach me and answer my prayers. I prayed many times that if He needed to get an answer to me that I wasn't getting, that He would send it to someone who loved me. And He did! Countless times my husband or the bishop or a friend would say something or e-mail me something and I would realize that was it! That was what I needed to know. That was the answer to my prayer, just delivered another way.

## Learning to Listen

Once we are open and receptive and are praying for learning, we then need to observe. Understanding and answers will come in a variety of ways so we need to be observant to find them. Even little things can teach us and inspire us. As we watch and listen, small whisperings will come.

For example, I needed to make a very important decision regarding my reconstructive surgery. While I was in the waiting room, two different women came in, each having had the different procedures I was contemplating. As I discussed their treatments with them, the answer for me was clear. It was a gift for me to be able to ask them questions and listen for the answers I needed.

Learning is everywhere around us, if we make the effort. Sometimes God has to be very literal and put it in writing for us to get the message. I personally have been inspired by messages found in unlikely places—including the back of a cracker box or inside a fortune cookie. Those moments of inspiration have led me to discover deeper and more personal revelation that the Lord wanted me to know. And while revelation doesn't usually come in a cookie or on a box, I believe that God will use a variety of ways to teach us. We need to be observant enough and open enough to learn.

## Learning from Others

A friend of mine, Wendy, related her "trying times" to me and shared some of what she had learned. She had been married in the temple but her husband was unfaithful. She had had multiple miscarriages; five of her children were wayward and involved in drugs. She struggled with health issues. And yet, she was learning in spite of (and perhaps because of) what she had experienced. She wrote to me and said, "Overall, they [her challenges] have helped me to become a woman of great faith and with a testimony of Heavenly Father's intimacy with each of us. I *know* He knows me personally and loves me (as He does each of us). I know that so many miracles have happened in my life because, even though I am a complainer sometimes, my faith has remained strong and firm in my Savior and the Atonement."[3] She has learned important things that the Lord needed her to learn.

Kayla, who has suffered through life with an adulterous, drug-addicted father, said, "I guess I operate on the belief that where much is required, much is given. Some of my most difficult disappointments have been such that I didn't know if I could continue in life. I wanted to stop and bury my head in the sand. But as I went forward in faith, trusting that, with Heavenly Father's help, I could learn from the experience, I have had amazing blessings and experiences. I know that I am a daughter of God and that as His daughter I can rely on Him for whatever strength I need to get me through any difficulty. My disappointments have stretched me as a person. I am less judging, a little more patient, and I have a deeper well of life experience to draw from to help others."[4] Her trying times have certainly led her to tremendous learning. As President Henry B. Eyring stated, the Lord will design these experiences for each of us to learn what we need to learn.[5] If we are willing.

## "Seek Learning, Even by Study"

We also can and should experience true learning through education as we go through our experiences. As I've been going through the experience of having breast cancer, I have taken steps to educate myself as much as possible. I have to say that the Internet is an incredible tool that has allowed me to learn invaluable information.

For example, each time I had a test or procedure, I would visit with my doctor and gain as much information as I could. Then I would go home and study as much as I could from the information I gleaned from the Internet. When I went back to visit with my doctor, I was loaded with information that helped me understand what was happening to me as well as having a list of new questions to ask.

One day, I was pondering over my decision about what type of reconstructive surgery I should have done. I discovered a video posted on YouTube of the type of surgery I had been thinking about. I was able to sit and watch a video of the actual surgery. Now, frankly, you have to have a pretty strong stomach for that, but I found the video to be absolutely fascinating. After a six-minute video, I had virtually all of my questions and concerns answered.

I mentioned my research to my plastic surgeon. He was absolutely thrilled. He said, "In the old days, we just told the patient what they needed to do and they said OK. And then we had to deal with all the aftermath because they didn't understand everything. I love it when a patient comes in having studied and learned so much. It makes treating them so much better, and they are a lot happier with the results."

Information can be so helpful as we face our trying times.

Learning can give us COURAGE. Often, when we first encounter adversity, we are afraid. We have a thousand questions: What will happen to me? to my family? What's next? How will I survive this? The scriptures remind us to "be strong and of a good courage, fear not, . . . for the Lord thy God . . . will not fail thee, nor forsake thee" (Deuteronomy 31:6). As we start to find answers to our questions, we can leave behind our fears and embrace courage.

Learning can help us MAKE DECISIONS. When we are as educated and informed as possible about whatever it is we are facing—whether it is breast cancer treatments or something else—we can start to see the big picture. Our confusion is lessened and we can understand what our options and alternatives are. And then we can make decisions with faith and courage, pursuing the best course of action for us and our families.

Learning can give us POWER. During my cancer treatments, I devoured information from all around me—the Internet, booklets, magazines, talking to other people who had gone through similar experiences—and I discovered that by gaining the knowledge for myself, I was able to become a partner with my doctors and take an active role in my own health care.

I remember going through radiation at the same time as three other ladies. As we chatted, the other three realized that they were often lacking in information. One would ask, "Why is your doctor choosing that treatment?" and the other would respond, "I don't know." They would often ask me questions and I would do my best to bring back information to them or guide them to the proper places to get their answers. As we all learned together, we were able to transform the way we approached our medical care and our comfort level with the entire process significantly improved.

## Spiritual Learning

Information. Education. Learning. All are critical in trying times. And all of it goes with us.

Whatever principle of intelligence we attain unto in this life, it will rise with us in the resurrection.

And if a person gains more knowledge and intelligence in this life through his diligence and obedience than another, he will have so much the advantage in the world to come. (D&C 130:18–19)

Not only do we have amazing secular knowledge available to us, but the amount of spiritual knowledge that is available is amazing as well.

Just think—we have all the scriptures, all the footnotes, an incredible amount of talks, a century's worth of conference talks, tons of church books, historical materials, maps, articles, and on and on. You want to study meekness? One search will reveal a wealth of knowledge right at your fingertips. Want to study Christ and His Atonement? A few keystrokes and your journey begins. We have a wealth of spiritual knowledge available to us, and the access of information is easier now than it has ever been.

Let's begin with President Henry B. Eyring:

Our first priority should go to spiritual learning. For us, reading the scriptures would come before reading history books. Prayer would come before memorizing those Spanish verbs. A temple recommend would be worth more than standing first in our graduating class. But it is also clear that spiritual learning would not replace our drive for secular learning. . . .

To keep spiritual learning in its proper place, we will have to make some hard choices of how we use our time. But there should never be a conscious choice to let the spiritual become secondary. Never. That will lead to tragedy. Remember, you are interested in education, not just for mortal life but for eternal life. When you see that reality clearly, you will put spiritual learning first and yet not slight the secular learning. In fact, you will work harder at your secular learning than you would without that spiritual vision.[6]

A commitment to learning will reap great rewards. As my family has experienced so many difficult things—political work, cancer, unemployment, selling our house, and more—becoming educated and informed has been a crucial component in navigating through our challenges. And drawing on the well of spiritual learning has deepened our understanding and increased our faith. The vast resources available to us are a great gift from God, but only if we accept that gift and choose to learn and grow.

CHAPTER 5

# Choosing to Fight and Win

Imagine, if you will, a war zone filled with buried land mines, hidden snipers, and camouflaged troops everywhere. Suddenly, a young child approaches the area and, oblivious to the threats all around her, begins to skip through. You watch in terror, your heart in your throat. Will she make it? Will she step on a land mine? Will a sniper mistake her for an enemy? You are consumed with fear for her. And yet you wonder: Can't she see what is all around her? Can't she tell this is a war zone?

I believe this analogy is a critical one for today. Many of us are navigating through our lives in the latter days naively unaware of the dangers surrounding us. We are ignorant of the incredible peril that we are in every day. And our children and youth are equally threatened and are often less aware of the spiritual threats around them.

We cannot discuss how to survive trying times without

discussing the individual who is out there fomenting and destroying all that is good. Satan is real; he is out there.

And we are at war.

# The Protect Marriage Amendment

The analogy of the war zone was never more apparent to me than in the battle in California to protect traditional marriage. As I mentioned, I had been an area coordinator for Proposition 22 that had been on the ballot nine years prior. We worked hard to pass a law that defined marriage as only between a man and a woman. Prop 22 was an unbelievable effort. And we won—significantly—much to the shock of those who opposed us.

But since that time, the opposition had been busy and had succeeded in convincing the California Supreme Court to overturn Prop 22. Immediately, the defenders of the traditional family went to work. It was truly amazing to see how fast things were organized politically. (I've been in politics a long time and I've never seen anything move that fast.) Prop 8 was qualified for the next November ballot.

Then the war began.

I was not exactly looking forward to being the regional coordinator for Prop 8 because I knew it would be a much, much harder battle this time and that the environment would be much, much worse. I felt a kind of kinship with Mormon, who spent much of his time fighting, but was so sad to have to do so.

Anytime you stand up for truth, you run the risk of being attacked. And attacked we were. Most everyone believed we would lose. I have to admit that there were times when I wondered about our chances myself. The barrage of media opposed to our cause was unrelenting. And a big change this time surprised me. When we worked on Prop 22, all the churches in our area except for two stood with us and helped us. As we contacted the various congregations in the area this time, minister after minister stated that they were unwilling to participate in the effort. They didn't want to "offend" their members. In fact, only a couple of churches besides The Church of Jesus Christ of Latter-day Saints got involved in our community. The landscape had certainly changed dramatically.

The entire nation watched and waited.

Personally, I prayed and worked and worked and prayed. Hundreds and thousands of volunteers stepped forward. I have never before witnessed such courage. They stood on street corners with their families, waving signs and enduring the truly hateful reactions of others. They canvassed neighborhoods, bravely sharing the message of truth. They boldly put bumper stickers on their cars and planted signs in their yards.

But let me tell you, Satan was abroad in the land. He and his forces were organized and working hard. I saw evil, firsthand.

Families with children had things thrown at them. People were attacked with water and rocks. Cars were damaged. Yard signs were repeatedly stolen or mutilated. Some people were followed. Others were threatened with the loss of their jobs. Some even had their businesses boycotted. An elderly couple was beaten up. And the language that was hurled at these faithful men and women and children was appalling.

And yet they stood strong, shoulder to shoulder, and marched forward valiantly. Right through the war zone.

The first question I asked when I came out of anesthesia after my surgery on election day was, "Prop 8? Did we win?" I shall never forget that moment. My husband drew close. "Merrilee, we won. We did it. We have won!" I laid back in my bed and wept.

Truth had prevailed. It was close. But truth had once again won.

# The War in Heaven

Gary Lawrence helped lead the battle advocating for traditional marriage in California as the professional political consultant. In the midst of the battle, he wrote a terrific article entitled, "Wonder What the War in Heaven Was Like? Watch California This Fall." In it he stated:

> "There was a war in heaven," my dad said as he taught me about our pre-earthly existence and the purpose of life. It had only been a few years since he had returned from service as a Marine in World War II, so it was natural that his 10-year-old son immediately imagined a great battle with planes, tanks, and bazookas. What a war it must have been, I thought.
>
> How disappointed I was when he told me the implements of that special conflict were . . . words.
>
> Words? How exciting could *that* have been? I liked my version better.
>
> But I soon grasped the importance of this hinge event in our existence and the "weapons" we used to defend the principle of agency and God's plan for the happiness of His children. And I grew to understand that this war has not ended, that only the battlefield has changed.[1]

The war has not ended. It is ongoing, right here, right now. Satan and his followers are here (Revelation 12:7–9). And they have not stopped fighting for the souls of men. Elder James J. Hamula explained:

> You have come into the world at a most significant time. We are entering the final stages of a great war. This war commenced before the foundations of the world and has been pursued with awful consequence throughout the world's history. I speak of the war between the followers of Christ and all those who deny Him as their God. . . .
>
> It was Satan who instigated this premortal war. . . .
>
> Unfortunately, Satan's war did not end with his expulsion from heaven. As John observed, Satan and his followers were "cast out into the earth" and have come here with "great wrath." The evidence of their wrath can be seen in the blood and horror that has afflicted man from the beginning of time.
>
> So profound and extensive have been the wounds suffered among men that God Himself wept as He surveyed man's condition.[2]

Many of us bear the wounds of the battle that is raging in the world today. Some of these wounds are seen and some are unseen.

As we experience trying times, we must be ever vigilant and watch for Satan's influence. If we do not, we will be susceptible to his buffetings, and our trials and challenges will be greatly increased.

We must stay aware. We must choose which voice we will follow.

## Satan's Plan of Misery

Brigham Young stated that "the Lord Jesus Christ works upon a plan of eternal increase, of wisdom, intelligence, honor, excellence, power, glory, might, and dominion, and the attributes that fill eternity. What principle does the devil work upon? It is to destroy, dissolve, decompose, and tear in pieces."[3]

Satan has a plan for us, and it's certainly not one we want. Many people have called it "Satan's Plan of Misery." President Henry B. Eyring, then a member of the Quorum of the Twelve, declared, "Satan wants us to be miserable as he is."[4]

His goal is not only our misery, but his ultimate goal is our *enslavement.* The Lord declared that Lucifer's intent was to destroy the agency of man. Greg Wright, author of *Satan's War on Free Agency,* writes,

> Accountability, or stewardship, was the principle which we fought to preserve in the War in Heaven, although scripture uses the word *agency* to describe it. The problem for us is that this war has come to earth and Satan's plan has not changed. It is not choice, but agency, that is once again under attack. His method is to get us to focus more on the enticements of our choices than on the results those choices can bring.[5]

Elder D. Todd Christofferson said,

> Satan has not ceased his efforts "to destroy the agency of man." He promotes conduct and choices that limit our freedom to choose by replacing the influence of the Holy Spirit with his own domination. Yielding to his temptations leads to a narrower and narrower range of choices until none remains and to addictions that leave us powerless to resist.[6]

The scriptures are replete with descriptions of Satan's plan. His goals are clear.

> Wherefore, men are free according to the flesh; and all

things are given them which are expedient unto man. And they are free to choose liberty and eternal life, through the great Mediator of all men, or to choose captivity and death, according to the *captivity* and power of the devil; for he seeketh that *all men might be miserable* like unto himself.

And now, my sons, I would that ye should look to the great Mediator, and hearken unto his great commandments; and be faithful unto his words, and choose eternal life, according to the will of his Holy Spirit;

And not choose *eternal death,* according to the will of the flesh and the evil which is therein, which giveth the spirit of the devil power to captivate, to *bring you down to hell,* that he may *reign over you* in his own kingdom. (2 Nephi 2:27–29; emphasis added)

For behold, at that day shall he rage in the hearts of the children of men, and *stir them up to anger* against that which is good.

And others will he *pacify, and lull them away into carnal security,* that they will say: All is well in Zion; yea, Zion prospereth, all is well—and thus the devil cheateth their souls, and leadeth them away carefully down to hell.

And behold, others he *flattereth* away, and telleth them there is no hell; and he saith unto them: I am no devil, for there is none—and thus he *whispereth in their ears,* until he grasps them with his awful chains, from whence there is no deliverance. (2 Nephi 28:20–22; emphasis added)

Behold, he [God] changed their hearts; yea, he awakened them out of a deep sleep, and they awoke unto God. Behold, they were in *the midst of darkness;* nevertheless, their souls were illuminated by the light of the everlasting word; yea, they were encircled about by the bands of death, and the *chains of hell*, and an *everlasting destruction* did await them. (Alma 5:7; emphasis added)

Did you catch all of them? Let's review them again:
- Misery (2 Nephi 2:16–18, 27)
- Bring us to hell (2 Nephi 2:27)
- Captivity (2 Nephi 2:27)
- Eternal death (2 Nephi 2:27)
- Rule over us (2 Nephi 2:27)
- Stir us up to anger (2 Nephi 28:20)
- Pacify and lull us into carnal security (2 Nephi 28:21)
- Flatter us (2 Nephi 28:22)
- Whisper lies to us (2 Nephi 28:22)
- Bind us with the chains of hell (Alma 5:7)
- Darkness (Alma 5:7)
- Everlasting destruction (Alma 5:7)
- Loss of freedom—personally and politically (Ether 8:25)

And these are only a few examples from the scriptures. It is crucial that we are aware of Satan's Plan of Misery. I find it amazing how much information has been revealed in modern scripture regarding Satan's plans for us. I believe that the Lord is clearly preparing us for the latter days, when Satan and his minions will be organized and aggressive in their war. Satan and his followers are unrelenting.

We must never forget that Satan is at war with the Saints (D&C 76:29)—with *us*. So often we read about Satan's plans and his goals and think they only apply to those outside of the Church. But we, as the saints of God, have merited his undivided attention. We are his target. And he has an individualized, personalized plan of misery for you and for me. We must be informed and aware if we are to survive the attack.

Do we ever have anger against that which is good? Do we ever look at others who are attempting to live the gospel and stand in judgment of their efforts in order to justify our own lack of effort? Do we passively attend church each week, lulled into security, believing that all is well and that we are immune from attack? We must be vigilant to survive.

As I look back at our lives over the past year, it is obvious that some of the things we experienced were the result of the plan of evil unfolding around us. Every day during our battle to protect traditional marriage taught us another lesson about Satan's efforts and the reality of evil.

It seems as though when we are experiencing trying times, we feel Satan's buffetings more keenly. We can be weakened and fatigued as a result. It is during these times when we are feeling at our weakest that Lucifer's followers are especially on the attack. But it can be hard to keep our minds and hearts focused when frankly, we're just trying to survive!

The Lord has not left us helpless, though, to suffer Satan's attacks. He has given us a surefire way to stay safe, stay protected, and even to fight back.

## Following the Prophet

It is not easy to live in the latter days. When we are in vulnerable circumstances, it is critical that we hold tight to the iron rod. We must be wholly committed to the gospel and to following the prophet. I have seen many people who did not have this commitment in their lives drift or fall away completely. The losses are tragic.

President Henry B. Eyring, then a member of the Quorum of the Twelve, discussed the choice we face.

> When we reject the counsel which comes from God, we do not choose to be independent of outside influence. We choose another influence. We reject the protection of a perfectly loving, all-powerful, all-knowing Father in Heaven. . . . In rejecting His counsel, we choose the influence of another power, whose purpose is to make us miserable and whose motive is hatred. We have moral agency as a gift of God. Rather than the right to choose to be free of influence, it is the inalienable right to submit ourselves to whichever of those powers we choose. . . .
>
> . . . The failure to take prophetic counsel lessens our power to take inspired counsel in the future. . . .
>
> Every time in my life when I have chosen to delay following inspired counsel or decided that I was an exception, I came to know that I had put myself in harm's way.[7]

Clearly, following the prophet will lead us to safety and keep us squarely within the influence of our Savior. Listening to the prophet and acting on his counsel offers us the protection we need to survive the trying times of the latter days. The prophet stands on the watchtower and shows us the way. It is up to us to follow with trusting obedience.

We cannot afford to ignore, argue with, or reject the counsel that is there for us. President Boyd K. Packer, then a member of the Quorum of the Twelve, said,

> Obedience to constituted priesthood authority will protect us from going astray. . . .

The doctrines will remain fixed, eternal; the organization, programs, and procedures will be altered as directed by Him whose church this is. . . .

But this we know. . . . The Lord organized His church to provide for mortal men to work as mortal men, and yet He assured that the spirit of revelation would guide in all that we do in His name. . . .

. . . We know His voice when He speaks.

Revelation continues with us today.[8]

I, too, add my witness. There is safety in the gospel of Jesus Christ. There is safety in following the priesthood leaders of His Church. There is safety in drawing close to our Lord. Author Emily Freeman writes:

In this fight, we do not have the luxury of "standing down." . . . One of our greatest strengths comes from *knowing* our Captain. . . . [President Howard W. Hunter said,] "We must know Christ better than we know him; we must remember him more often than we remember him; we must serve him more valiantly than we serve him." In doing so we will become fully converted and able to fight for what we believe.[9]

Christ can and will save us. He has sent us the prophets and apostles to be His voice. There is safety in heeding their counsel. As we struggle with adversity in our lives, our only security and peace lies within the truths we have and the covenants we have made. Time and time again, I witnessed the faithfulness of those around me who had tied themselves securely to their Savior and His Church and His prophet. They were anchored. And they and their families were safe when the storms raged and howled over their heads.

The good news of the gospel is that the righteous will win the war! But that does not mean we won't experience pain and conflict along the way to ultimate victory. We battle the efforts of the Ultimate Bad Guy on a daily basis. So it makes sense that we must learn everything we can on how to win. By understanding Satan's plan for each of us, we are better equipped to fight back. By turning to the scriptures and the counsel of our leaders, we can arm ourselves to defeat the forces of the Adversary and come off conqueror.

If we choose to fight with the Lord by our side, we will win!

CHAPTER 6

# Choosing to Love, Listen, and Fill Our Lives with Light

Clearly, some of the trying times we suffer through are because of the efforts of Satan, and some are from the choices we make as a "natural man." Satan's methods are carefully constructed to increase the suffering and misery in our lives so it's important that we are aware of his methods and learn ways to combat them.

- He will tempt us to sin.
- He will try to discourage us.
- He will constantly distract us.
- He will darken our world.

By understanding Satan's plan for each of us, we are better equipped to fight back. And we can fight back by making choices to repent, to love, to listen to the Spirit, and to fill our lives with light.

# Sin

First of all, what would be a discussion of Lucifer's methods without talking about sin?

President Henry B. Eyring, then a member of the Quorum of the Twelve, writes:

> There is an opposing power. It is the power of sin, and it is visibly accelerating. I will not try to bring examples to your minds. The media and what you see in the lives of those around you present you with tragedy enough. And even in your experience, you surely must sense the ominous increase of toleration and even encouragement of the powers of sin to corrupt and torment.[1]

Let's admit it. We mess up. Rather regularly. And messing up causes a lot of pain in our lives. I suspect that's why the Lord is always advising us against it. But it sure is hard to look at ourselves carefully and own up to the sins we're hanging on to.

I gotta admit—my opinion of my own sins has changed rather dramatically this last year.

I was told that I was dying. That's pretty much what it means when the doctor tells you that you have cancer: "You are dying. We'll try to stop it, but right now, you have death in there."

All of a sudden, you see the rest of your life, however long that may be, in fast forward. You instantly visualize yourself standing before the Savior and being asked to account for your life. And you shrink.

I had a few days to contemplate that possibility. My time could be up. This could be it. The end of mortality. Right now. And the image of me, standing before the Lord, was on freeze-frame. As I contemplated what that moment meant, I took a very hard, very honest look at my life. In a short while, I could be standing before my beloved Jesus.

In those moments of introspection, I realized there were stains on my soul. Sins that I had been holding on to that I didn't want to hold on to anymore. I shrunk in horror to even consider approaching the Lord with those sins on my hands. My perspective changed in an instant, and my only desire was to appear before the Lord cleansed and washed clean.

I began to repent, redoubling my efforts to have His Atonement apply in my life. No way was I going to hang on to those sins for one more second—not even the really "small" sins. I'm happy to say that some have been completely abandoned and I have not picked them up again. (I am sorry to say that a few are still hanging around. I am not perfect, after all.)

Righteousness always is happiness. And the Lord wants us to be happy. So in order to be happy, we must repent, because repentance is the best weapon we have against sin.

## Choosing to Repent

Recently I flipped the page of my daily scripture verse and read Doctrine and Covenants 19:15: "Therefore I command you to repent—repent, lest I smite you by the rod of my mouth, and by my wrath, and by my anger, and your sufferings be sore—how sore you know not, how exquisite you know not, yea, how hard to bear you know not."

I thought, *What is with all this repent, repent stuff anyway?* (I did mention that I had a few sins hanging around, right? Let us just say "pride" is proving to be quite stubborn . . . ) My thoughts continued,

*It isn't like I'm going around all the time doing seriously bad stuff. Why the constant call to repent?*

Thankfully, the Lord is patient with me and my pride issues.

The call to repentance is actually the call to change our behavior. It is God's way of saying, "Your behavior is not to the level it can and should be." Repentance is an invitation to compare our behavior to the Savior and to keep that which is *holy* and that which is *wholly* true to our spirits and our destiny and to shed the bad behavior that doesn't fit. As Greg Wright wrote, "The pure in heart are those whose beliefs are a higher priority than their behavior. They continually seek to modify their behavior, conforming it to their beliefs."[2]

In the sacrament prayers, we covenant to always remember Him. I've gained great understanding over the past few years of the importance of remembering His Atonement. We should remember not only the way He suffered and died for us (and by so doing, stop sinning), but we should also remember how He lived (and by so doing, do that which is good and holy).

Repentance is that process of always remembering Him and constantly adjusting and modifying our behavior. When we repent, we turn back to God and keep making our way toward Him. We remember Jesus Christ and we strive to become like Him.

Repentance takes constant, daily effort, but as we do it, we will be spared many afflictions that would otherwise be ours. That alone is worth every effort.

We all go through challenges in our life from the simple to the extreme. Commitment to our Savior and His commandments is the one sure way to survive them. Because temptation to sin is one of Satan's major methods, a firm foundation in righteousness with daily fine-tuning repentance is critical.

The scriptures show that righteousness is a major weapon against the Adversary:

> And because of the righteousness of his people, Satan has no power; wherefore, he cannot be loosed for the space of many years; for he hath no power over the hearts of the people, for they dwell in righteousness, and the Holy One of Israel reigneth. (1 Nephi 22:26)

I love those words—"Satan has no power."

To add this method of defense to our personal arsenal to fight Satan's influence, I recommend doing a daily affirmation—a positive statement that you say every day to set your course of action for the day. It is important that these affirmations be written down so that you can see them visually. It's also important that you say them out loud so you can hear them. I like to add a little movement as well so I often recite my daily affirmations with a dance, a jump, a cheer, or a rock-out session!

Our first daily affirmation is:

*Each day I choose to be obedient and to repent of anything that doesn't lead me to the Savior.*

Go ahead and write that affirmation on a card or Post-It note and put it in a prominent place. And each morning, read that statement out loud with enthusiasm. You will be amazed how often you will hear the words repeated in your head throughout the day, encouraging you to choose righteousness and to undertake an immediate course correction for any behavior that falls short.

# Discouragement

Elder Kevin W. Pearson said, "Chronic discouragement leads to lower expectations, decreased effort, weakened desire, and greater difficulty feeling and following the Spirit. Discouragement and despair are the very antithesis of faith."[3] Is it any wonder, then, why discouragement is one of Satan's favorite and most powerful methods of attack?

It is easy to become discouraged. These days, all you have to do is watch the news! To see if discouragement is affecting your life, ask yourself these three questions:

1. Do I feel depressed or frustrated much of the time?
2. Do I find myself saying, "Well, I don't want to get my hopes up . . ."?
3. Do I feel like saying, "What's the use?"

I can remember one week when my husband was hoping for an interview with a potential employer. We were discussing the possibilities and he said, "Well, I don't want to get my hopes up." We agreed that that was a good idea. But then I got mad.

"But I *want* to get my hopes up!" I declared. "I've always kept my hopes up!"

"I just don't want us to be disappointed again," Steve replied.

"I know, I know," I said. "But I'm telling you, I *want* to get my hopes up!" We literally had had nine months of bad news of all kinds and we were to the point of hoping for just one week without bad news!

We were so very discouraged. Even now it is hard not to be discouraged. The economy is terrible. Almost no one is hiring. This is our family's third round of lengthy unemployment. I have to say that we're struggling with this challenge! And looking at those three questions, I have to answer, "Yes, yes, and YES!" And that's not good!

## Choosing to Love

So how can we combat discouragement? With love!

Love may seem unrelated to discouragement, but I would argue to the contrary. Let me share some examples to explain.

There was a time when one of my sons was struggling. To outward appearances, he was rebellious and hostile, but I knew that in his heart, he was discouraged with himself and with his life and his choices. Every day he seemed to radiate the feeling of "What's the use?"

One day he was particularly hostile and the very powers of darkness seemed gathered around him. He was standing in his bedroom with anger emanating in waves out of his eyes. I was standing at the door, desperate to pierce his walls of discouragement and hostility.

I spoke quietly but firmly. "Son, I love you. I will always fiercely love you, no matter what. And your Daddy loves you dearly too. And I know that your Heavenly Father knows you and loves you. Jesus loves you—He has suffered and died for you because He loves you so much. You are surrounded by love. Just know that it is there for you, and it is real."

He looked down and when he looked up again, he had changed. The anger had cooled, and I could see a glimmer of hope in his eyes. "I know, Mom," he said quietly.

I can testify that love has a powerful effect on discouragement.

And love has that effect on us when we fill our own lives with it, despite whatever discouragement we may be feeling.

I received an e-mail from a friend who donated an organ to a person in need and had grown in understanding of love. He says,

> Whenever an individual sacrifices for people or principles which benefit people, I believe a few things almost invariably happen: (1) True sacrifice will be real. We'll get an opportunity to pay what we offered, accompanied with all the challenges. There won't be any relieving influences that take the pain away nor will the consequences of the sacrifice be removed. (I don't breathe easier because I donated a lobe of my lung versus lost it to smoking.) (2) Evil will always oppose good. (3) Greater love will always enter your life when you make choices to sacrifice and love others, an understanding of that love doesn't come to us in any other way. (4) You will always feel the love of your Heavenly Father for you in a very personal way. I can never see this young woman—in any environment—without feeling the love of Heavenly Father in my life and feeling a deep love for her and her family. I always have tears (embarrassingly) and I always feel a deep debt of gratitude for what I was permitted to do.[4]

Powerful love has the capacity to defeat Satan. Every single time we choose love, we fight against him. Every time we choose to be kind, forgive, reach out, or care, the powers of the Adversary are weakened. As love begins to permeate our lives and reach into the very fiber of our being, we become more and more immune to the temptations and efforts of Lucifer and his minions of misery. It may seem like such a small, basic thing to do, but every act or thought of love reduces Satan's power over us and over those we love.

It's easy to love those we love, but harder to love our enemies. When I was publicly betrayed in a city council meeting by someone I thought was a friend, I found it hard to extend love to her. The day after the meeting, I woke up still upset; I was practically spitting venom!

Then I turned over my daily scripture verse and burst out laughing. The verse read: "Be patient in afflictions, revile not against those that revile. Govern your house in meekness, and be steadfast" (D&C 31:9).

Now, you have to admit that sometimes the Lord has a major sense of humor. I laughed and laughed and told my husband that the Lord was speaking to me in a way I couldn't mistake. It was time to let go of the venom and choose love. Easy? No. But definitely the better course of action. I had enough burdens already; I didn't need to strap another one to my back.

The Prophet Joseph Smith connected love's ability to combat the forces of the Adversary when he said, "To be justified before God we must love one another: we must overcome evil; we must visit the fatherless and the widow in their affliction, and we must keep ourselves unspotted from the world."[5]

Sometimes when we're facing challenges or difficulties, we let the love in our life slip. We're tired. We're angry. We're frustrated. And feelings of love and caring are often put on the back burner while we focus on the negative emotions of our situation. But we need to do the exact opposite.

It is crucial in these times to tap into the love of our Savior, the source of the greatest love in our lives. So many times I was faced with pain and sorrow and bad news upon more bad news and I would go to a quiet place and plead, "Father, I need to feel love right now. That's all I ask. I just need to feel love." Oh, and when I asked for that love, I could almost physically feel the Savior enveloping me in His arms and reassuring me. That love would just be there, like a warm, comforting blanket. It was the one thing I needed most to help me take another step and hold my head up.

That love is there for you. Ask for it. It is right there.

Once we have felt such love, it's much easier to let that love flow through our lives to touch the people around us. Sharing love is absolutely the best medicine in the world.

During my cancer treatments, I would drive to the doctor's office day after day but before I left my car, I would pause and say to myself, "Now, Merrilee, this is a wonderful opportunity to share love." And I would hop out of my car with my head held high and my heart full and ready to share. I would actively seek to share love with every person I encountered. I would radiate a beaming smile to every person in every elevator and every hallway. What a difference it made to walk those corridors filled with love instead of with fear and sadness!

And, oh, the waiting rooms! What a wonderful place to share love!

One day in particular stands out. I had had my surgery and was at the breast surgeon's office for my three-month checkup. The waiting room was absolutely packed with women. There was definitely a feeling of fear in the room. I started with the lady next to me.

"So, what have they got you in here for?"

She chuckled. "Lumpectomy. Next week." We chatted about her situation and I could tell others began to listen in.

"Wow, that's terrific that they caught it early and you can just have a lumpectomy!"

She smiled and brightened. "Yeah, I guess so."

"You're gonna do great!" I said. "You'll be just fine." I could see the burden lifting.

The woman across the room spoke up and asked me, "When did you have your surgery?"

I related the sad tale of woe of having my surgery on election day while I was a candidate, complete with some jokes to lighten the story.

"So you're the one!" she said. "They had to move my surgery for a big one, they said. I had my surgery later that afternoon."

The whole room got a kick out of that story.

Pretty soon everyone was talking and the receptionist was smiling. All except one woman.

"So, my new *breast* friend," I began. (That's our running joke with each other.) "What's your story?"

She related how she had had cancer a few years ago and had gone through everything—surgery, chemo, radiation, the works—but that the cancer had come back. The doctors had told her that it was very serious and that it may be terminal. Her husband had passed away, and she was absolutely devastated.

"I'm not sure I even want to fight it," she said. The sadness and discouragement in her voice was overwhelming. The room grew quiet.

I jumped up out of my seat. "That calls for a group hug," I declared and ran to hug her. The whole room drew close.

"Tell me about your cancer," I said. And as she did, I kept reassuring her: "Oh, they have a good treatment for that" and "You can handle chemo again." Finally, I looked her in the eye. "You can fight this," I said. "They have wonderful new treatments. You just have to have faith. However many days you have left, you can fight for life. I know you can. We all know you can." All the women in the room murmured expressions of love and support.

Just then her name was called and she stood, more confident, more courageous.

When it was time for my appointment, the receptionist stopped me in the hallway. "I love it when you're here," she said. "You always run a wonderful therapy session out there in the waiting room. The women need that." I thanked her and went into my room. I waited for a very long time—but I'm always willing to wait for terrific doctors!—and when my surgeon came in, she was smiling. She came over to me and took my hand.

"I want to thank you," she said. "You have done an amazing thing today. I just met with the woman from the waiting room. With tears in her eyes, she told me what you did for her. She said you gave her the will to live. I have to thank you. You always bring such incredible love here." And with that she gathered me in a big hug. We were both pretty misty-eyed over that one.

Again, love is the answer. Even if you are the one in great suffering and need, sharing love can lighten your own load like nothing else can. Sharing even little tiny bits of love throughout your day and throughout your experience is transforming.

I now am able to understand Christ's statement better:

> Come unto me, all ye that labour and are heavy laden, and
> I will give you rest. Take my yoke upon you, and learn of me;
> for I am meek and lowly in heart: and ye shall find rest unto
> your souls. For my yoke is easy, and my burden is light.
> (Matthew 11:28–30)

I have learned that His burden is light because He fills every moment with love. And truly, love can lift every burden and ease every care.

Our daily affirmation for this most wonderful weapon against the Adversary is:

*Each day I fill my life with love. It guides my every thought and every action.*

There is power in choosing love. It is the power that will shield us from the darts of the Adversary.

# Distraction

If I had to pick one of Satan's methods that is the most effective on me personally, it would definitely be distraction. He doesn't always need to get us to sin. He can just distract us from doing what is essential.

In the Relief Society in our ward, we've done a lot of surveying to gather good information to help us plan. The number one excuse for not doing visiting teaching? People are too busy. The number one excuse for not attending the temple? People are too busy. In fact, busyness is by far the leading problem for the sisters in our ward. They are distracted. And they are not the only ones.

Elder Kevin W. Pearson, in discussing Satan's methods, stated,

> Discouragement leads to *distraction,* a lack of focus. Distraction eliminates the very focus the eye of faith requires. Discouragement and distraction are two of Satan's most effective tools, but they are also bad habits.[6]

I thought it revealing that he called them bad habits. Truly they are that.

Mormon discusses the methods Satan used to attack the Nephites:

> Now the cause of this iniquity of the people was this—
> Satan had great power, unto the stirring up of the people to do
> all manner of iniquity, and to the puffing them up with pride,
> tempting them to seek for power, and authority, and riches,
> and the vain things of the world. And thus Satan did lead away
> the hearts of the people to do all manner of iniquity. (3 Nephi
> 6:15–16)

The devil is very good at leading away the hearts of the people
by using "the vain things of the world." Such things were distracting to the Nephites, and they are still distracting us today. Are our
hearts on the things of the world or on the things of God?

The devil and his annoying ones are always at work, distracting us. The flashy, glittery things of the world catch our attention
and shift our focus. I'm always amazed that I can find time for my
favorite TV show, but I have to squeeze in my scriptures. Time
with our families falls short as we are distracted by sports, yet
another party, work, and yet another activity that we've signed up
the kids for. The radio, TV, newspapers, and Internet cry, "Lo
here, check this out!" or "Lo there, you should pay attention to
this!" Sometimes the steady, quiet drumbeat of righteousness that
comes from the Spirit is drowned out by the screaming cacophony
of the world around us. All the devil has to do is shift our attention away from that which is good and he has succeeded.

When considering the level of distraction in our lives, consider these helpful questions:

1. Am I often too busy to do the most important spiritual
things?

2. Do I find myself in a rush much of the time?

3. Do I find my mind is consumed with things of the world?

# Choosing to Listen

Listening is absolutely crucial if we are to survive the latter days. We cannot and will not survive without developing this important skill.

There are two parts to listening. First, it's important that we *not* listen to Satan. (That would be a good idea, don't you think?) Satan loses his power over us if we don't pay attention to him. The scriptures offer some important guidance on how to do that. In discussing how Christ handled Lucifer's attacks, the scriptures teach us that "He suffered temptations but *gave no heed* unto them" (D&C 20:22; emphasis added). And Lehi's vision of the tree of life contains the same clue: "And great was the multitude that did enter into that strange building. And after they did enter into that building they did point the finger of scorn at me and those that were partaking of the fruit also; but we *heeded them not*" (1 Nephi 8:33; emphasis added).

Here is our key: When it comes to Satan, we should heed him not! Pay no attention!

In the movie *The Wizard of Oz,* Dorothy and her friends finally reach the fabled Wizard. But then Toto pulls aside the curtain and Dorothy notices that the Wizard is not who he appears to be. He begs, "Pay no attention to that man behind the curtain." Unfortunately, the truth is exposed. He continues to speak into the microphone, his voice booming: "I am the great and powerful . . ." Then, when he realizes it is useless to continue his masquerade, he speaks in a normal voice, finishing with, " . . . Wizard of Oz."[7]

Dorothy and her friends can see the Wizard for who he is— a regular person completely lacking in superhuman anything. His power to intimidate or control them completely evaporated. The same holds true for Satan. We are so much more powerful than he is or ever will be. We just don't realize our power. He has no body. He has no access to the Spirit. He is weak—as long as we don't give him any control over us. If we heed him not, he has no way to directly influence us.

So your friend wants to gossip and sling dirt. Pay her no heed! Your coworker wants to tell dirty stories. Pay him no heed! Your spouse wants to rent an R-rated movie. Pay him no heed! It seems such a simple idea and yet it is so powerful and effective. Do *not* listen to the influences of Satan that come in any way, shape, or form.

The second part of listening is to learn to listen to the Lord. In order to do this, we must have *quiet* in our lives. That can be a little challenging for most of us. It isn't that we don't want to listen to the Lord, it's that we're distracted. We're busy, busy, busy and we don't have the quiet or take the time to commune with Him.

Certainly it's a challenge to make time in our lives to listen to the Spirit. But if we don't, the cost is great. Can you imagine trying to land a jumbo jet without hearing the directions from the air traffic controller? Can you imagine going through life without hearing from Him who knows us best? It would be impossible. At the very least, we would be wandering through spiritual land mines without a clue.

Quiet listening can bring the peace we so desperately need in trying times.

Relief Society General President Julie B. Beck counseled us on the importance of listening for personal revelation to guide our path when she said,

We can do the work of the Lord in His way when we seek, receive, and act on personal revelation. Without personal revelation, we cannot succeed. If we heed personal revelation, we cannot fail. The prophet Nephi instructs us that the Holy Ghost will show us "all things what [we] should do." It was prophesied that in the latter days the Lord would pour out His Spirit upon His handmaids. This will happen as we allow ourselves to be still enough and quiet enough to listen to the voice of the Spirit.[8]

We must not heed Satan; we must heed the Spirit.

To combat distraction, we must learn to listen. When I was struggling so much with so many things, my daily prayer walk with the Lord was my lifeline. It was my time to walk along, albeit rather slowly sometimes, and tune out the world and tune in the Spirit. Each of us needs to carve out a special time each day. The Lord wants to talk to us—especially when we are suffering. But we will not be able to hear Him unless we quiet ourselves.

Elder James J. Hamula counsels us:

> Learn to hear the voice of the Lord. His is a still, small, and whisper-like voice. It is one that is felt more than it is heard. It comes in the form of thoughts, feelings, and impressions. To hear such a voice, you must be still and quiet in your own soul, laying aside your excess laughter and light-mindedness. While it may not seem easy to so discipline your life, hearing the precious, loving voice of the Lord will sustain you in every circumstance and is therefore *worth every effort.*[9]

Our daily affirmation for listening will be:
*Each day I will have some quiet time so that I may listen intently to the Lord.*

# Darkness

"For they love darkness rather than light, and their deeds are evil, and they receive their wages of whom they list to obey" (D&C 29:45). This verse is disturbing to me. I don't want Satan paying my wages! But it is clear that Satan is darkening our world just as fast as he can.

One look at the world—the media, the pollutants, the entertainment, the decline in moral values—and it's clear that Lucifer is busy turning down the dimmer switch. Elder Neal A. Maxwell noted, "Hard choices as well as passing through periodic mists of darkness are needed in order to maintain life's basic reality—that we are to overcome by faith."[10] Those "mists of darkness" may be a necessary part of our mortal experience, but they are also frightening.

I remember many years ago having a discussion with my Grandma Faulkner. I mentioned having seen a movie recently and how disturbed I was that it had some surprising and bad things in it. Grandma Faulkner told me of the time she saw *Gone with the Wind* when it first came to the theaters. It was a huge deal—quite the major epic production—and she was excited to see the movie. She recalled,

> I remember sitting in the audience and it came to that big moment when Rhett is going to leave Scarlett. She clings to him, wailing, and asks him what she is to do with herself. He stops and turns and says [I shall paraphrase], "Frankly, Scarlett, I don't give a darn." [But we know which swear word was used instead.] The whole audience gasped and we sat back in our seats. We had never, ever heard a swear word in the theater before and it was shocking. There were pickets and letters to the editor and a big hullabaloo over it all. Times have changed now.

I remember thinking that was so silly. But it certainly illustrates how dramatically things have changed. Just think of this past week. How many swear words have you heard on a screen? How many immoral acts have been presented as acceptable? How much violence have you seen? The world is certainly darkening at a rapid pace.

I received a letter from a concerned parent who had attended a lecture of mine and had gone home to investigate the behavior of her children. She did not like what she found. She wrote:

> Dear Sister Boyack:
>
> I guess why I am sending this to you is so that maybe during your lectures you could inform parents of [a popular social networking site]. It is awful. It is evil. It is BIG. . . . Satan really is a hard worker and wants to steal the innocence and beauty of our children. He has nestled himself in a perfect battle position.

What an apt description of the Adversary—he is not only in battle position, he is on the attack.

As we consider Satan's method to bring darkness to our world, let's consider the following three questions:

1. Compared to five years ago, is my environment darker and more negative?
2. What media am I allowing into my life?
3. On average, are my thoughts negative or positive?

## Choosing to Fill Our Lives with Light

President Dieter F. Uchtdorf said,

> How often do we find ourselves surrounded by threatening clouds and stormy weather, wondering if the darkness will ever

pass? If there were only a way for us to lift ourselves up from the turmoil of life and break through to a place of peace and calm.[11]

There is!

When we are in crisis, the powers of darkness can seem overwhelming. Several times, I experienced spiritual self-doubt where I thought I had received inspiration and things didn't turn out the way I had expected. I felt like I was groping in the darkness with no clue of where to go. It was a very, very difficult time.

Thinking of right and wrong in terms of light and dark can be helpful. Sometimes it makes the choices so much clearer. Is this light? Or not?

Elder Jeffrey R. Holland spoke of the best way to combat the darkness we encounter:

> The promoters of darkness often seem to have direct access to the media microphone. We may not be able to take that away from them, but we can at least raise our own voices. We can teach correct principles often and in as many ways as possible.
>
> Since darkness is the absence of light, surely the most powerful way to counter darkness is to fill the world with light.[12]

And Elder Robert D. Hales agreed:

> Light and darkness cannot occupy the same space at the same time. Light dispels darkness. When light is present, darkness is vanquished and must depart. More importantly, darkness cannot conquer light unless the light is diminished or departs.[13]

Filling our lives with light will greatly protect us from the attacks of Satan. Doctrine and Covenants 93 is a wonderful section to read and reread as we ponder on the topic of light:

And that I am the true light that lighteth every man that cometh into the world; . . .

Behold, here is the agency of man, and here is the condemnation of man; because that which was from the beginning is plainly manifest unto them, and they receive not the light.

And every man whose spirit receiveth not the light is under condemnation. . . .

The glory of God is intelligence, or, in other words, light and truth.

Light and truth forsake that evil one.

Every spirit of man was innocent in the beginning; and God having redeemed man from the fall, men became again, in their infant state, innocent before God.

And that wicked one cometh and taketh away light and truth, through disobedience, from the children of men, and because of the tradition of their fathers.

But I have commanded you to bring up your children in light and truth. (D&C 93:2, 31–32, 36–40)

We must be willing to "receiveth" the light. This dovetails with our willingness to listen to the Spirit. Each of us has the choice of inviting more and more light into our life each day. These choices have a powerful, protective effect on us and our families. When we choose the light, darkness *must* dispel.

Doctrine and Covenants 84 also discusses the importance of light:

And I now give unto you a commandment to beware concerning yourselves, to give diligent heed to the words of eternal life.

For you shall live by every word that proceedeth forth from the mouth of God. [There's that important "listening" part.]

> For the word of the Lord is truth, and whatsoever is truth is light, and whatsoever is light is Spirit, even the Spirit of Jesus Christ.
>
> And the Spirit giveth light to every man that cometh into the world; and the Spirit enlighteneth every man through the world, that hearkeneth to the voice of the Spirit.
>
> And every one that hearkeneth to the voice of the Spirit cometh unto God, even the Father. . . .
>
> And by this you may know the righteous from the wicked, and that the whole world groaneth under sin and darkness even now.
>
> And your minds in times past have been darkened because of unbelief, and because you have treated lightly the things you have received. (D&C 84:43–47, 53–54)

Truly we live in a time of much darkness and sometimes we find ourselves engulfed and overwhelmed. By actively seeking to invite light in our lives, we will literally be able to see our way clear.

How can we seek after light? One way is unswerving dedication to the prophet. He has access to light and truth every day and we can follow his light. I learned this principle so clearly during the days of working to support the traditional marriage amendment. Those people who had made the decision to follow the prophet—no matter what—were solid. Their families and their faith were secure.

Those people who had not made that decision were confused, frustrated, and rather miserable. They made poor choices. Their families were lost and confused. And several of them fell away, lost in the darkness.

Setting a family rule of "We follow the prophet—no matter

what!" can help lead the family to light and keep them safe. Elder Jeffrey R. Holland commented further, "We need to set and enforce family rules that protect us and our children from those who would sneak into our homes and there replace light with darkness."[14]

We must also continue in our commitment to personal faithfulness. This commitment can invite light into our lives on a daily basis. Sometimes, it's clearer to ask the question, "Is this leading to light or leading to darkness?" than asking, "Is this good or bad?"

Heavenly Father and Jesus Christ are sources of light. As we grow and develop spiritually, are we becoming sources of light? Are we a source of light to our children? To those around us?

Elder Richard G. Scott encouraged us with these words:

> You know what is right and wrong. Be the leader in doing right. At first, you may not be understood. You may not have the friends you want right away, but in time, they will respect you, then admire you. Many will come privately to receive strength from your spiritual flame. You can do it. I know you can do it.

> When your life complies with the will of the Lord and is in harmony with His teachings, the Holy Ghost is your companion in need. You will be able to be inspired by the Lord to know what to do. When needed, your efforts will be fortified with divine power. Like the missionaries, you can be protected and strengthened to do what alone would be impossible.[15]

Think of darkness, and then the impact of one speck of light. Darkness cannot prevail against it.

Our Savior has promised us that He is the Light. He has

promised us that He will lead us to the light and away from darkness. As we are grappling with our troubles and challenges, His promise is one we can depend on.

Our daily affirmation for light is this:

*Each day I seek after light. I choose light over darkness. That choice guides all my decisions.*

# Daily Affirmations

Remember our daily affirmations? Shout them out with me:

Each day I choose to be obedient and to repent of anything that doesn't lead me to the Savior.

Each day I fill my life with love. It guides my every thought and every action.

Each day I will have some quiet time so that I may listen intently to the Lord.

Each day I seek after light. I choose light over darkness. That choice guides all my decisions.

As we fight Satan, we must always remember our divine destiny. President Henry B. Eyring, then a member of the Quorum of the Twelve, declared, "Your birth at this particular time was foreordained in the eternities."[16] You have incredible power to overcome Lucifer. You can and must win this war in your own life. You were saved for such a day as this. And you can win.

The Lord Himself has reassured us that He will fight for us: "And I, the Lord, would fight their battles, and their children's battles, and their children's children's, until they had avenged themselves on all their enemies, to the third and fourth generation" (D&C 98:37).

We will win the war against Satan with the Lord by our side. We will be victorious as we seek the Savior and stand against Satan, nothing wavering.

May we fight well.

CHAPTER 7

# Choosing to Nourish
# Body and Soul

On March 10, 2008, I was on my prayer walk. I had finished my prayers and was just bebopping along down the road. I soon became aware that the Spirit was calling my name, so I slowed down and focused my mental energies on listening. I was given much instruction that was very helpful to me. And then I was told something rather startling. My journal records what happened:

> You must take better care of your body. (What???) Yes, you must take better care of your body. Your healthy body is needed to do the work of the Lord and you have not been taking good care of it. Start NOW. Take care of your body better.
>
> I will be with you so that you are able to do all that you are asked to do. You will have the ability you need to fulfill your special mission.

I was rather shocked. I didn't understand at first. After all, wasn't I out exercising? And I had been making a big effort to eat my fruits and veggies like a good girl. But as I thought about it, I realized I was also consuming a *lot* of junk. I love to eat and eat a lot. At first, I decided I would give up all junk. Then I realized that I would probably blow up if I did that.

So I thought, *Well, I can keep track of ten things in my mind. So I'll give up ten things.* So on the spot I gave up cake, candy, cookies, chips, pie, brownies, ice cream, shakes, soda, and fries. Yes, indeed. This sounded like the perfect challenge for a Perfect Year. (I often undertake an exercise in self-discipline and try to do something perfectly for 365 days in a row. If I mess up, I just start again). So I began on that day.

And I almost croaked. I had no idea how much junk I had been eating! The hand-to-mouth reflex was incredible. But I persevered. Not one bite of anything on my Top Ten list hit my lips. Not one. After two weeks, my body and brain calmed down a bit. I stuck to it.

Now I know you're dying to know: How much weight did I lose? Not one ounce. I do not lie. Sure, I had about twenty extra pounds to spare, but I did not lose one ounce. Still, I could not deny that the Spirit had directly prompted me to take better care of my body. I had put forth a lot of effort into my Perfect Year, so I kept going.

When breast cancer hit six months later, I thought, *You've GOT to be kidding me! I'm behaving more healthy now than I ever have in my life!*

I shall never forget the day I finally understood the miracle. I had had my surgery and was in the surgeon's office for a follow-up visit. She told me that the tumor had turned out to be much larger than they had originally thought—it was 2 inches—but it had only spread to one lymph node. Then she put her hands on my shoulders and looked directly into my eyes. "You may now thank your body for doing an amazing job fighting off this attack. It's a miracle," she said. In that instant, I heard the Spirit say, "*That's* why." And I knew. If I had kept my old eating habits, I would have fed the cancer and quite possibly would have died. It was truly a miracle.

I thought I needed to be healthy and fit to do some big project. But no. I needed to be healthy and fit to survive breast cancer! And by listening to the Spirit, I was in a position to be able to fight it off and live to serve.

I am not telling you that you should do the same thing. Each of us must make our own decisions with respect to our body and our health. But it is still a good idea to evaluate our own body/spirit connection.

## Nourish Our Bodies

The Lord explained the connection between mind and body in Doctrine and Covenants 88:15: "And the spirit and the body are the soul of man."

We cannot be perfected or glorified unless the body and the spirit are permanently joined together! We must not nourish our spirit and neglect our body, or the other way around. Both are integral and essential.

Elder Russell M. Nelson has said,

> Your faith must also be nourished. Enrich that faith with private scriptural study and with exposure to other fine books, art, and music. Nourish the gifts of the Spirit on the same daily basis that you feed your physical body.[1]

Lucifer understands this truth. He makes a great effort to damage or break that spirit and body connection by tempting us. He tried to tempt Jesus to satisfy the needs of His body. But Christ, of course, rejected such temptation (Luke 4:2–3). We, too, can fight back by making a commitment to nourish our bodies, keeping them strong and healthy. We must learn to care for our bodies and control our passions so that we are fit for service in the Lord's kingdom.

I have to admit, after a lifetime of incredibly good health, I certainly took my body for granted. I hadn't truly understood the intense symbiotic relationship between my body's fitness and health and my ability to receive spiritual guidance. During my chemotherapy, I needed to take so many medications. It was incredibly difficult to be receptive to the Spirit with a foggy mind and a sick body. It was especially difficult because I desperately needed the Spirit's direction at that time in my life.

I once had a conversation with my friend "Jenny," who suffers from many serious health conditions. After our conversation, I understood better how hard it is for people who are dealing with chronic health conditions to maintain a high level of spirituality. You're just trying to get out of bed and get dressed each day! Survival is your top priority. As I went through chemo, I was shocked at how much harder it was to concentrate on scripture reading, commune while I prayed, and stay in tune. I was so focused on keeping my tummy quiet that it was hard to think of anything else!

No matter what our circumstances are with our body— despite its size, shape, or condition—each of us can commit to nourish it. Our body is an incredible gift from God. But it requires constant attention.

I like focusing on the word "nourish" rather than getting detoured with words like "diet" or "exercise" which can conjure up all kinds of reactions. Now, when I look at what's going into my mouth, I ask the question, "Will this nourish my body?" That question is a revelation! It doesn't mean we have to go hard-core and eliminate anything that is not macrobiotic or organic. We can instead focus on what will feed us in a positive way. The same question applies for moving our bodies every day. Am I nourishing my body's fitness?

Promptings will come throughout the day. And as we hear them, we can respond promptly! I am alive today because of a choice I made about my body. I encourage each of you to begin listening to those persistent little thoughts that come to you regarding your body. You never know the miracle that may be yours if you do.

## Remember to Replenish

I remember rushing the children one day and having a son ask, "Why are we in a hurry, Mom?" I couldn't answer. "I don't know," I barked. "But hurry up!"

Consider these words that have become so common in the description of our lives: stressed, hurried, rushed, busy, overscheduled, and MORE STRESS.

Now I must admit that facing death brought all of my rushing to a screeching halt! I instantly began to reevaluate *everything* that I had been in such a hurry to do.

I came to a sad realization: I am less of a human BEING and more of a human DOING. (I'm afraid that's what will be left on my tombstone—"Here lies Merrilee Boyack. She sure got a lot done!")

You know what my all-time favorite activity is? Crossing things off my to-do list!

So what was I supposed to do now that I was facing the possibility of the end of my to-do list? Frankly, I was so busy just *surviving* that I didn't have a chance to make any lists. But I did have a chance to stop and ponder. You have lots of time to ponder while you're waiting for doctor after doctor.

I realized that I had to take care of myself. I was no good to anyone dead. Nor are you. Like they say in the instructions on the airplane, "Oxygen to the adult first!"

I also realized that stress could literally kill me. When you examine any of the big health killers—heart disease, cancer, autoimmune diseases, etc.—all of them have a *huge* element of stress impacts. And yet we go on being overly stressed. That isn't dumb—it is practically suicidal!

I remember taking an online stress analysis test. The high stress score was 300. If you scored more than 300, you had an 80 percent chance of contracting a fatal condition. My score was 625. It was a miracle I was alive! Now, granted, most of the stress was not my own doing. But still, I realized I was having to process an enormous amount of stress, and I had to deal with it. Taking care of myself moved right to the top of my to-do list. In fact, it was pretty much the only thing on the list!

As I looked at my life, I realized that I had been doing a good job of "taking care of myself." I exercised faithfully. I always made sure I got enough sleep (well, except during chemo!). I drank lots of water and I watched my nutrition carefully. I had regular doctor visits and all the scheduled tests. I even took care of myself in mental health ways: a regular weekly date night with my husband

and regular playtime with my friends. I had been making a lot of effort for many years to take good care of myself.

But . . . I needed to step it up a notch. I needed to go *beyond* the basics. I needed to de-stress and *replenish*. But how was I to do that? What did I need to do or stop doing? My old behavior was not enough. What should I do now?

## Nourish Our Soul

My pondering coincided with the new year. I had had my second chemo treatment on New Year's Eve and was now free from having to fix my hair every day, so I had time to think. Every year I choose one thing to work on all year. What would be my goal for this year?

Now frankly, I was in the middle of chemo and my brain was mushy. I was in survival mode. But I kept praying and pondering.

After the fourth chemo treatment, the Lord took pity on me. One day I was lying in my beloved bed and feeling a bit nauseous. I reached over the side of my bed for the box of Wheat Thins that was there. I was munching along when—Eureka! There it was!

On the back of the box—"Nourish Your Soul."

That was the answer! It wasn't enough just to take care of myself. I had to take it one step further and *nourish my soul*. I knew from the scriptures that my soul was my body *and* my spirit.

After I read the slogan, it would not leave my mind. It has become a *passion*—a quest. And also a fight.

How was I supposed to nourish my soul? I knew what I was supposed to do, but I didn't know how I was going to do it.

Shortly after this experience, my visiting teachers came to visit. After some chitchat, Becky asked me a question: "So, after facing this huge life experience with breast cancer, how have you changed? What have you changed in your life?" I pondered that for a while and admitted that I hadn't really changed a thing— yet. At that point, I was simply surviving.

But her question nagged at me. I thought, *If I go through all this and don't change a thing, what good was it?*

So, what have I changed? Well, I can say that I have devoted much more energy to nourishing my body. But more completely, I have pondered and worked on nourishing my *soul.*

## Follow Jesus' Example

One day I was thinking about Jesus and I realized something very enlightening. (Frankly, I thought about Him a *lot.*) I remembered that He liked to go off and spend time by Himself. I got out my scriptures and began to search.

Before His formal ministry began, Jesus "was led up of the Spirit, into the wilderness, to be with God" (JST Matthew 4:1). Jesus had gone out into nature to commune with His Heavenly Father. For a long time. To prepare.

Jesus also had good friends, including the twelve apostles and Mary, Martha, and Lazarus, who He liked to spend time with. The scriptures record that He

- Attended wedding parties (John 2:2)
- Sang a hymn (Matthew 26:30)
- Prayed alone (Luke 9:18)
- Went up a mountain to pray (Luke 9:28)
- Went to the Mount of Olives "as he was wont" (Luke 22:39)
- Walked by the seashore (John 21:4)

- Went to the garden where "Jesus ofttimes resorted thither with his disciples" (John 18:2)

We recall the Garden of Gethsemane with sadness. But for Christ, it was a place of rejuvenation, a place of love. He went there often.

Jesus had a habit of spending time restoring His soul. Think about that carefully. Imagine if you will, *His* to-do list. And yet even with the most important to-do list in all of eternity, He still took time to nourish His soul.

Take the time. If it was important for Jesus, it should be important for us.

Making the nourishment of our spirit a high priority helps us navigate the challenges that face us in our lives. And we need to start doing it now. Once major challenges hit, it's very difficult to go around filling your lamps or your tanks or whatever you're using for light and power! By then, you're out of energy!

I cannot begin to emphasize how critical it is to have good spiritual habits in place. That's why I hesitated on answering my visiting teacher's question about major changes in my life. I have worked hard (with prior Perfect Year experiments) to make prayer and scripture study an absolute daily habit in my life. Attending the temple weekly had also become a regular habit. I am so profoundly grateful that those foundation stones were already in place when I needed to rely on them the most.

It's never too late to start putting those stones in place! Today's the day! Just pick one goal and give it relentless effort. Do not procrastinate. Nourishing your spirit must take priority and is worth the effort.

## Lift the Quality of Our Lives

I read an article in the *Ensign* that profoundly changed my perspective.

Elder Douglas L. Callister wrote,

> If we could part the veil and observe our heavenly home, we would be impressed with the cultivated minds and hearts of those who so happily live there. I imagine that our heavenly parents are exquisitely refined. In this great gospel of emulation, one of the purposes of our earthly probation is to become like them in every conceivable way so that we may be comfortable in the presence of heavenly parentage and, in the language of Enos, see their faces "with pleasure" (Enos 1:27).
>
> President Brigham Young (1801–77) said, "We are trying to be the image of those who live in heaven; we are trying to pat[t]ern after them, to look like them, to walk and talk like them." I would like to peek behind the veil that temporarily separates us from our heavenly home and paint a word picture of the virtuous, lovely, and refined circumstances that exist there.[2]

That idea intrigued me greatly. What was our heavenly home like? How were the people "exquisitely refined"? How did they behave? What did they do with their time? What were their surroundings like? I was filled with questions as I pondered that vision. And a looming question was, "How do I get from here (my life now) to there (that quality of life)?" Or to ask it more simply, "How do I get from turmoil to tranquility?" for that surely sounded like the most tranquil of circumstances. Turmoil I have; tranquility I want.

## Seek After Virtue

As I pondered Elder Callister's article, ideas began to come. First, I thought of the thirteenth Article of Faith. Specifically the part that reads, "If there is anything virtuous, lovely, or of good report or praiseworthy, we seek after these things." I love those words. Virtuous. Lovely. Praiseworthy. I should be actively seeking those kinds of things. Seeking seemed to imply a much more active pursuit than occasionally hoping something good passes my way.

Next, I turned to my scriptures, thinking on that word "virtue." I turned immediately to one of my favorite verses: "Let thy bowels also be full of charity towards all men, and to the household of faith, and *let virtue garnish thy thoughts unceasingly;* then shall thy confidence wax strong in the presence of God; and the doctrine of the priesthood shall distil upon thy soul as the dews from heaven" (D&C 121:45; emphasis added).

Again this seemed to be encouraging an active pursuit. The word "unceasingly" implies that it should be going on all of the time. My very thoughts, not just my behavior or surroundings, must be garnished with virtue.

Sheri Dew, in speaking at the World Congress of Families, noted the critical importance of virtue in the way we live our lives. She said,

> No society can be stronger than the moral fiber of its people. There is power in virtue. Said Clare Boothe Luce: "There can be no public virtue without private morality. . . . And there cannot be a good society unless the majority of individuals in it are at least trying to be good people. . . . A nation that is traveling the low road is a nation that is self-destructing. It is doomed, sooner or later, to collapse from within."
>
> Virtue, *especially* moral virtue, builds strength of character.

A lack of virtue damages one's moral compass until ultimately that person can't be trusted.[3]

That clinched it. I resolved to use *virtue* as a filter in my life. It was a small change, but one that garnered huge results. I encourage you to try it for just one day. *Is this virtuous?* My, how my TV viewing changed. *Is that virtuous?* I guess I really don't want to spend a lot of time being gossipy in my head. On and on it went. Using virtue as a filter has caused my life and my behavior to be more refined in a very short amount of time. And frankly, I feel so much better! It is amazing what good, clean, living will do! But not just good and clean. Taking the next and higher step of including virtue has been an incredible and powerful experience. President Gordon B. Hinckley said,

> The challenge to recognize evil and oppose it is one that every moral, virtuous person must accept.
>
> It all begins with our own personal virtue. Reformation of the world begins with reformation of self.[4]

While it was important for me to improve and learn to use virtue as a filter, I knew I needed to go one step further. It was not enough to weed out the bad, I needed to *add* those things that were virtuous and lovely into my life.

## Be Creative

I was able to take that next step as I pondered a talk by President Dieter F. Uchtdorf given at the September 2008 Relief Society General Broadcast. He spoke extensively about Godlike attributes and focused on creativity as one of them.

> The desire to create is one of the deepest yearnings of the

human soul. No matter our talents, education, backgrounds, or abilities, we each have an inherent wish to create something that did not exist before.

Everyone can create. You don't need money, position, or influence in order to create something of substance or beauty.

Creation brings deep satisfaction and fulfillment. We develop ourselves and others when we take unorganized matter into our hands and mold it into something of beauty. . . .

. . . Remember that you are spirit daughters of the most creative Being in the universe. Isn't it remarkable to think that your very spirits are fashioned by an endlessly creative and eternally compassionate God? Think about it—your spirit body is a masterpiece, created with a beauty, function, and capacity beyond imagination.

But to what end were we created? We were created with the express purpose and potential of experiencing a fulness of joy. Our birthright—and the purpose of our great voyage on this earth—is to seek and experience eternal happiness. One of the ways we find this is by creating things.[5]

As children, we were constantly involved in activities of creating—finger painting, playing with clay, creating plays for our parents, making up a silly song or story, inventing games, drawing with chalk, the possibilities were endless. Somehow, though, when we get older, we seem to think those activities are limited to those with "talent." To a large degree, we shut down our creative work as adults. So for me, President Uchtdorf's talk was a call to action. I remember thinking at the time that I was on massive overload and couldn't do much, but I knew I could do something.

As soon as I could, I went to the store and bought a few flats of pansies. I came home and planted them all over the front yard.

I thought they would be very cheery to see whenever I came home from the doctor! And they were! They brought me great joy.

But as I pondered his talk in light of nourishing my soul and seeking creativity, I was filled with ideas.

I noticed that the Mormon Channel had a new program called "Everything Creative," inspired by President Uchtdorf's talk. The show's purpose was to explore creativity through interviews with artists and creative people of all types. Each episode was unique because the interviewee from a previous episode became the interviewer of another creative artist. The list of interviewers was interesting: a musician, an architect, a painter, a professor and Egyptologist, a professional basketball player, a professional organizer, a mother, an author, a muralist, and a trading post owner. Clearly creativity is broader than we thought it was!

I asked some of my Internet friends the question, "How do you create?" Their answers were fascinating, ranging from writing music or playing an instrument, to sewing clothes and costumes, to undertaking cross-stitching or scrapbooking projects. Some people mentioned how much they loved to bake and be creative in the kitchen. Others counted making friendships as a creative experience. One of my favorite responses was this one: "I create with enthusiasm and integrity."

I was amazed and impressed with the variety of creativity in the lives of the people around me. Each is striving to add beauty and refinement and virtue to their lives and to the lives of others. And clearly, this provides refreshment to their soul.

## Turn to Others for Love and Support

As we experience trials and challenges, part of helping us nourish our soul is turning to others for love and support. I think this is one of the greatest hidden blessings of trying times. As we go through our challenges, we see firsthand the amazing, incredible support system that is available to us in our families, in our neighborhoods, and in the Church.

I'm not a big card keeper (sorry, family!), but when I realized that I might have some dark days ahead, I decided to keep all the cards people sent to me in a bucket. All I can say is WOW. I have been amazed at the goodness of others. People I've never met have sent e-mails with prayers and well-wishes. The support and love is unbelievable. I call my collection of cards my "bucket of love." Each day as I glance at that gigantic pile of cards it tells me one thing. Never, *ever* forget that you are loved. I feel as though I have truly experienced Zion—one heart and one mind knit together with love.

God sends us angels all the time to help us through our difficult times. Someone will give you a call, pat you on the arm at Church, tell you they love you. A neighbor will stop by and look you in the eye and ask how you're *really* doing. A coworker will offer to help.

Know this. People want to help you. They love you. They are there for you. It is important to let them help you. Remember, if they needed you, you would be there in a heartbeat. So turn to them. Lean on them. Their love and support will sustain you through your darkest times and bring light and love into your life when you are struggling to survive.

## Pray Always

One sure way to nourish your soul is through prayer. Personal prayer is powerful. I can testify to that truth. I've felt it. It is *real*. It is incredibly powerful.

And the prayers of others can amplify that power. Do you

know that others are praying for you too? They are. More than you know. On both sides of the veil. Never in my life have I had people praying for me so much, and I have felt the effects.

But it doesn't take hundreds and hundreds to tap into the power of prayer. I am convinced that one single, heartfelt prayer can access the powers of heaven.

Believe me, in that dark, quiet moment in the night when your heart cries out to your Father, *He will be there.*

The Savior is right there with you. He will wrap you in His arms of love. He will be with you every single step of the way.

We all know that God hears and answers our prayers. But do we really *know* that? I thought I did.

I knew my prayers were heard and answered, but somehow I kind of envisioned some angel secretary taking notes and forwarding on the really important stuff and delegating the rest to others to deal with. Maybe that sounds stupid, but it's how I imagined it worked.

Until one day I was reading a book and the author wrote,

> I am God's child. I have his attention all of the time. He loves me completely. . . . His love for me is unconditional and continual, and it is the consistent motivating force in his interactions with me.[6]

I read that and thought, *Yeah, I believe that.* But then my eyes went back and read it again: "I have his attention all of the time." I read it a third time and thought, *Wait a minute. How can I, personally, just me, Merrilee, have God's attention all of the time? He has billions and billions of children—and I'm just one person.*

And then I remembered the scripture:

> Thus saith the Lord your God, even Jesus Christ, the

Great I AM, Alpha and Omega, the beginning and the end, the same which looked upon the wide expanse of eternity, and all the seraphic hosts of heaven, before the world was made;

The same which knoweth all things, *for all things are present before mine eyes.* (D&C 38:1–2; emphasis added)

All things are present before God. He does not experience time in a linear fashion like we do. He sees everything. I knew that. But somehow I didn't know it really applied to me.

I have God's attention all of the time because all things are present before Him.

That means right now, while I'm praying, He's right there. Every moment, every time.

All of a sudden, my mind expanded with understanding. I have always loved my Heavenly Father. I have always felt Him close. But somehow, I hadn't truly realized that He was there, *always*—for me, just me.

Not only does God truly and literally hear all of my prayers, but He is right there with me in each and every moment. In my present.

It is an incredible idea. And one that has changed my life.

Truly, we can find tranquility in our lives as we nourish our body *and* soul. Adding beauty and loveliness and virtue and peace into our lives can be a lifelong pursuit. Such an unceasing pursuit will cause the dews of heaven to water our soul and bring us the nourishment we crave.

CHAPTER 8

# Choosing to Celebrate
# the Good

Mentally and emotionally, I understood the goal to nourish your soul. But actually applying it to life is a whole other thing! It's strange that something so important and so positive takes so much effort. But it should not be surprising in the midst of dealing with challenges, going to doctors, caring for the house, and a million other things that are part of life, that it takes major effort to ratchet your life up a notch.

One day I was contemplating how to put what I had learned about nourishment into my life. I kept thinking "How?" and "What?" with few answers. I was very hot that day and decided that I would cool off in the Jacuzzi. Most people turn up the heat on the hot tub, but I was already cooking from the inside out so I needed to cool my body's furnace a bit.

As I sat in the cool water with the jets running full tilt, I began to think again of nourishment.

Nourish. What did it mean? I thought of other words. Replenish. Rejuvenate. Restore. Feed.

What did those words have in common? Maybe it was because of where I was sitting, but they reminded me of a spa! Places of calm and beauty where there is a whole lot of rejuvenating going on.

Do these "spa" words have a place in our lives? Are we replenishing ourselves? Are we rejuvenating our bodies? Are we restoring our minds and emotions?

I let my mind wander down that track. Do I have a *life* spa? That question started me thinking about spas in a whole new way: S.P.A.—Special Positive Activities.

I wondered what Special Positive Activities I could incorporate into my life that would nourish my soul.

I thought deeply of those things that brought virtue, loveliness, and refreshment to my life. Indeed, the minute I thought of the phrase "anything virtuous, lovely, of good report or praiseworthy" I thought of the arts and music.

There it was! The key to how to apply these things into my life. As I thought of them, I came up with these S.P.A. areas: Art, History, Music, Exercise, and Nature (AHMEN, for short).

These are the things that restore my soul. You may have others, but these are the ones that spoke to me.

# Art

Elder Douglas L. Callister in his talk of the beauty of our heavenly home spoke of the "art of heaven."[1] I pondered the art in my home and realized—to my surprise—I only had one picture! One!

The rest was kid-art or word art, but there was only one piece of what would be characterized as "fine art."

Then I thought back to my youth. My mother had planned a trip to Europe. For years she saved quarters in milk jugs so she and my dad could go on a trip when the kids were older. The time came and my parents realized that they could take my younger brother and me along and go camping for the same price as the two of them going and staying in nice hotels. The trip was on!

My mom decided we needed some education before we spent five weeks touring art galleries and cathedrals throughout Europe. She decided we would use our family home evenings to prepare. She bought a beautiful, large book featuring the best art of Europe. Interestingly, I still have that book in my home thirty-five years later!

For more than a year, we focused on the various artists of Europe during each family home evening. We studied their famous works and learned their stories. Week after week, after our regular lesson, we would study together. Each of us took turns studying an artist and presenting the information to the rest of the family. Those lessons have remained with me and cultivated a love of art within me that has lasted my whole life.

Think of the inspiration that went into a Renoir, a Michelangelo, a Degas! Think of the light and intelligence that flows from such inspiration.

Elder Douglas L. Callister said, "The nearer we get to God, the more easily our spirits are touched by refined and beautiful things."[2]

Connecting with the arts in a variety of ways would indeed be nourishing to my soul. There was just one problem. I'm not very artsy. (Pablo Picasso lamented, "Every child is an artist. The problem is how to remain an artist once he grows up."³ Amen!)

So what could I do? How could I have an art S.P.A.—Special Positive Experience—activity in my life?

First, I tried to sign up for a class to learn how to make mosaics. I adore mosaics and figured any art that consisted of breaking and cracking things had merit. Unfortunately the class was cancelled due to lack of interest. Undaunted, I signed up for a class that offered a variety of artistic experiences. Again, the class was cancelled.

I really wanted to add art back into my life but it was proving to be a challenge! One day I decided to look on iGoogle. Eureka! I found the Smithsonian Art Gallery application for my computer desktop. Best of all, it was free! My computer suddenly became my own personal gallery. Since I spend a lot of time on my computer, I can see beautiful art of all kinds all day long. The program also often has a little snippet about the artwork or the artist.

It's strange how something so small and easy has become a major source of enrichment in my life. I cannot begin to tell you the impact that looking at beauty and interesting art has had on my life. I had no idea how starved I was! I'm like a sponge, soaking it up.

## DESIGN YOUR PERSONAL S.P.A.: "How can I incorporate an Art experience into my life?"

Ideas may include going to an art museum. (When I go, rather than looking at everything, I like to pick three works of art and sit and ponder them for a long time.) You could watch a DVD, work on decorating your home with beauty, take a class at your local college or community center, or buy some watercolors or clay. Be creative. There is art all around us.

As we bring art into our lives, we will become more refined like our heavenly parents and our homes will reflect beauty.

# History

This may seem like a strange one to focus on, but I find that the study of history provides a rich texture of understanding and perspective to our lives. It can nourish our soul in its own unique way.

When my husband, Steve, lost his job, it was a very difficult time. It was hard to deal with this on top of the discouraging news every day and the depressing economy both nationally and for our family personally. At the time, Steve happened to be reading several historical biographies by David McCullough: stories of John Adams, Teddy Roosevelt, Harry Truman, and others.

After reading through many of the books, Steve commented, "I cannot believe how many times each of these great men lost everything they had and had to start again. And not just one time, but for many of them, over and over. They had to start from scratch. And they would. They would begin again and fight to improve their lives. I can do that." It was incredible how the study of history brought inspiration, hope, and nourishment to his life.

We studied together the story of the daughter of John Adams and her experience with breast cancer. We had no idea that she had had cancer and we were clueless about how they treated it back then. We ended up feeling enormous gratitude for the blessings of modern medicine that were ours as we faced a similar situation.

Think of the stories from our history. Can I find tranquility and peace when I study?

Have you suffered the loss of an infant? Read the story of Emma and Joseph Smith. Do you suffer from a disability? You can gain great motivation by studying the story of Helen Keller and her teacher, Anne Sullivan. Are you grappling with fear? You would be inspired by the stories of the signers of the Declaration of Independence. Loneliness? Read the story of Eleanor Roosevelt. Do you want more courage and spiritual commitment? The life of Joan of Arc will thrill you.

### DESIGN YOUR PERSONAL S.P.A.: "How can I incorporate a History experience into my life?"

You could listen to a lecture online. (Ted.com offers some great stuff.) You could take a class, watch the History Channel, go to a museum, watch a DVD, buy a book of stories and read one a week. You could study or write your family's history.

I have a son who loves the History Channel. I shall never forget the day when I walked in the family room and my entire family (Dad and the boys) were watching TV. "What are you watching?" I asked.

They all looked up and enthusiastically responded, "We're watching the History of Cement. It's awesome!" OK, there's history and then there's history . . .

# Music

I love this quote by Berthold Auerbach: "Music washes away from the soul the dust of everyday life."[4]

Elder Douglas L. Callister said this:

If we could peek behind the heavenly veil, we would likely be inspired by the music of heaven, which is probably more glorious than any music we have heard on this earth. . . .

. . . Sift through your music library and choose primarily that which uplifts and inspires. It is part of the maturing process of your eternal journey. This would also be a fine time to learn a musical instrument or improve musical skills now partially possessed. . . . . .

Some events in life are so sublime that they cannot be imagined without the companionship of beautiful music. We could not have a Christmas without carols or a general conference without sacred anthems. And there could not be a heaven without music of surpassing beauty. President Young said, "There is no music in hell, for all good music belongs to heaven." It would be punishment enough to go to hell and not hear a note of music for all eternity.[5]

When I was fighting off the sadness and depression that accompanied my personal turmoil, I would often listen to Christmas carols at full volume. My husband would come in and say, "What in the world are you listening to?" I told him I needed some major cheering up! He thought I was crazy. But it worked!

After I made a commitment to nourish myself through good music, I began to do two things. First, I listened to more classical music both on my computer and in my car. I've found that there is nothing like Bach to order your mind when you feel frazzled. And the strains of Chopin are so soothing. What a difference it has made to my soul instead of listening to a daily dose of talk radio or the latest hits.

Second, I picked out five pieces of inspiring music to memorize and perfect on the piano. I play the piano, but like most everyone else, I haven't played it nearly enough. I decided that I wanted to commit my favorite classical pieces to memory so that they would always be mine wherever I was. Even my son caught the bug and began to work on a piece day after day, which surprised us all. "I just really love 'Claire de Lune,'" he commented. (I think it helped that a certain young woman really liked it too.)

Bringing beautiful music into our lives and into our homes has an enriching effect that can both increase the peace we feel and help us to endure trying times. An accomplished pianist and mother, Sally Peterson Brinton, shared her experience:

> I have learned that music can bless the lives of children, and in turn can richly bless the home. We are striving to surround our children with beautiful music, ranging from the classic composers to the rich heritage of our Latter-day Saint hymns. . . . How exciting it is to see our children choose the sacred hymns of the Church over songs heard on TV or the radio. As I watch our children gain appreciation for Beethoven and the other great masters, I'm convinced that it's not that they're musical geniuses, but simply that they are developing a love for beautiful music through constant exposure. For it is true that the more we become acquainted with good music, the more we enjoy and appreciate it. One is never too old or too young to enjoy good music; even a young baby loves the hum of a lullaby.[6]

On days where I felt too sick or tired to do anything, sweet, lovely music helped feed my soul.

## DESIGN YOUR PERSONAL S.P.A.: "How can I incorporate a Music experience into my life?"

Of course, you could purchase some inspiring music CDs or download some uplifting songs. But I would urge you to take it a step even further and pick a specific day or time to listen to music so that it becomes a regular part of your life. You could attend a concert—schools and colleges offer so many musical programs at extremely reasonable prices (or even for free!). If you play a musical instrument, pick it back up! If you've always wanted to try one, now is the time to start.

# Exercise

Moving our bodies and being committed to fitness is crucial not only to nourish our body, but also our soul. I learned to exercise from my mother who spent many hours in front of the television with soup cans in each hand working out to Jack LaLanne, one of the first televised exercise gurus. (Mom is now 88 and walks three flights of stairs four times a day in addition to a mile walk around the senior living facility she lives in. She is in amazingly great shape.)

I, too, have exercised for years, taking a daily prayer walk that is quite lengthy and productive as I live in a hilly area. But now I wanted to step it up a notch. I wanted more. What I needed was variety.

I was also inspired by the activities of those around me. My friend Dana rides her bike all over town. My friend Marty loves to hike and backpack. My son Brennan is an avid mountain biker. And I love to see the old man at the club where I take my yoga class who swims every day. All have incorporated movement and exercise in their lives to nourish their bodies.

I find as I move my body, my mind is invigorated. After each surgery and chemo treatment, I longed to go outside and get moving again. To begin with, I could usually only make it up the street a few houses but each day I was able to do a little bit more. I am so thrilled to be able to walk a long distance again. And now I'm mixing up my exercise routine—I bought both a yoga DVD and a kick-boxing DVD. I figure both will do a great job in helping me de-stress!

## DESIGN YOUR PERSONAL S.P.A.: "How can I incorporate an Exercise experience into my life?"

We can begin by observing others and copying what they do. Or, better yet, we could join them! You could purchase an exercise DVD or join a class. Bottom line, make it a goal to *move* each day. Try one new method this month and add a variety of movement into your life.

# Nature

After my surgery, I *craved* going outside. I would just stand on the front porch and inhale! One day I asked Steve to take me to the beach. I remember that day with such joy. I sat there, all bundled up, just looking and listening and feeling. Oh, it was glorious! The sunset, the waves, the sounds of the roaring surf, the seagulls soaring overhead. I drank it all in to restore my achy soul.

A brother wrote of his experience with nature:

I awoke before sunrise, as I always do when camping. . . . I walked alone a short distance from camp to the top of a rocky knoll. The area was remote: the nearest paved road was more than 20 miles away, the nearest settlement more than 50. From where I stood, all that was visible was untouched by human hands. Around me, sharp-edged white boulders were interspersed with juniper and occasional blossoms of cacti and globe mallow. Ahead of me, a serene shadowed valley gave way to ridge after purple ridge of mountains stretching toward the growing dawn. Directly behind me, a towering peak of white rock caught the orange blush of sunrise.

There was a certain timelessness to that moment—waiting for the sun to clear the distant crest of the Wasatch Plateau. I could imagine a time even more ancient—a time when no mortal eye had viewed that scene—when perhaps even the hosts of heaven surveyed the landscapes of the newly prepared earth with gratitude, wonderment, and awe. . . .

That sunrise was, for me, an intensely religious experience. . . . The feeling of wonder for the gift of this earth I derived from that experience is one I will never forget.[7]

Nature can truly restore our souls. As we go through trying times and everything seems to be in chaos, we can stop and take a few moments to breathe in fresh air, let our faces be warmed by the sun, and gather strength to face another hour. It can bring us great tranquility in the midst of turmoil.

I absolutely love to go camping and be outdoors. Because of all my medical challenges, though, this has not been possible so I've had to experience nature in smaller bits. But as I've stayed aware of how important nature is in my life, those bits have been restorative. Even sitting in the waiting room, waiting for the doctor, I gaze out the window to see the flowers and trees and hills around me. I try to eat lunch outside whenever I can. Simple things. Simple, and yet it is so wonderful to tap into the beautiful earth that God has provided for us.

## DESIGN YOUR PERSONAL S.P.A.: "How can I incorporate a Nature experience into my life?"

Sometimes it's simple. Start by eating lunch outside from time to time. Take a walk and really notice the beautiful flowers and plants and mountains and sky. Breathe deeply! You could add hiking or camping or boating to your vacation plans. Go to a beautiful park or quiet place to ponder. Plant flowers! Sit on your porch. Stop and watch the sunset. Dance in the rain. Go to the lake or beach or river. Collect rocks and bring them into your home.

Connecting with the power of creation can nourish our soul in deep ways that will make a difference in the quality of our lives.

## Finding Tranquility and Peace

We are in the midst of turmoil. But we can gain tranquility and peace as we nourish our souls. Christ set the example of rest and rejuvenation and even had His favorite garden where He went to refresh Himself.

We can lift the quality of our lives through seeking virtue, exploring creativity, and nurturing our spirits. We can apply these things in our lives with our own personal special positive activities. I've mentioned the areas that nourish my soul, but you can pursue your own. Even a tiny effort yields wonderful rewards.

Tranquility and peace come as we are true to who we really are and as we draw closer to our Heavenly Father and our Savior.

Each of us is on a personal quest to become like our heavenly parents. As we take these next steps to become more lovely, more refined, and more virtuous, the entire nature of our being will rise. And as we nourish our souls, we will be better able to handle whatever comes our way.

CHAPTER 9

# Choosing to Let Go and Heal

As I was going through my treatments, I repeatedly felt impressed to start taking yoga. Now I have to admit, I was not thrilled about this idea. I've tried yoga before, and have been invited to leave the class.

But over and over the idea of a yoga class kept coming to my mind. I had read studies that showed the positive effect of yoga with breast cancer patients. But ultimately, what I realized was that, while I had been able to process massive amounts of stress in my youth, I'm getting a little older. I needed to have mechanisms in place in my life to help me handle the stress that was yet to come. Yoga fit the bill.

I went to class the first day. It was a class held for breast cancer survivors by Team Survivor. I met the instructor, Susan; she's from Persia and knows all about chakras and energy and everything. She was very sweet. She began by having us lie down on our mats on our backs in a completely relaxed position. Then she began to speak softly and gently as she guided us in first "noticing" our body and then "relaxing" our body.

It was one of those life-changing moments where time stood still.

I realized that my entire body was a bundle of stress. I was recuperating from radiation and had ended up with a frozen shoulder that was giving me great pain. But bit by bit, I was able to relax each part of my body. I don't know how I would describe it exactly except that as I did, I experienced joy.

And Susan's voice—oh, that voice!

"It is good that you are here. You are good because you are here. You can handle anything." Then she begins with the toes—that's my favorite. "Notice your toes, all ten toes. Wiggle your toes. Be happy for your toes." I'll tell you, I've never loved my toes so much as I do in yoga! They're fantastic!

On and on she goes. Each part. "Notice your legs, the top of your legs, your knees, your calves. Now let them go." I imagine myself lying in a calm pool of water as my legs float away. "Notice your hands. Make a fist. Now relax them and let them go."

Over and over she intones. "Let it go. Let it go. Are you feeling any stress? Any anger? Let it go. Just let it go."

The yoga class centers my whole body and soul for the entire week. All week long whenever bad things happen, I hear Susan's voice in my head, saying, "Let it go." And miraculously I can.

For days and weeks, I listened to Susan's voice: "You are here right now. You do not have to think about tomorrow or yesterday. You are good right here, right now. Be good to your body. You love your body. You take care of yourself. You love yourself."

It took me a while to realize what was happening. I was healing. Truly healing.

# Healing Now and Later

Healing has taken on new meaning in my life, as you might imagine. The words from my blessing, "You will be completely healed through your faith," have reverberated through my life. I have clung to those words.

Even the word "healing" has gained great power for me. Each day I would pray for healing. I would pray over the various body parts that weren't doing so well. I even began to pray for healing of every cell in my body, head to toe. But then I decided that I had better pray for healing down to the subatomic level! I finally settled on asking for healing of both body and spirit.

And one day, when I was lying on a table in a doctor's office, I just knew. I was healed. I was completely healed. The cancer was gone. I was so deeply, deeply grateful.

But I didn't feel all better the next day.

As I pondered how I felt, I realized that I had experienced trauma through every bit of my being. And even though my body was healed of cancer, my heart was still wounded and hurting. I was still dealing with so much—the aftereffects of treatment, the pain of Steve's unemployment, the stress of selling the house—that my emotions and my spirit were still *not* healed.

Elder Richard G. Scott, whose life has had many challenges with losing two little children and his wife in death, relates his understanding of healing:

> It is important to understand that His healing can mean being cured, or having your burdens eased, or even coming to realize that it is worth it to endure to the end patiently, for God needs brave sons and daughters who are willing to be polished when in His wisdom that is His will.

Recognize that some challenges in life will not be resolved here on earth. Paul pled thrice that "a thorn in the flesh" be removed. The Lord simply answered, "My grace is sufficient for thee: for my strength is made perfect in weakness" (2 Cor. 12:7, 9). He gave Paul strength to compensate so he could live a most meaningful life. He wants you to learn how to be cured when that is His will and how to obtain strength to live with your challenge when He intends it to be an instrument for growth. In either case the Redeemer will support you. That is why He said, "Take my yoke upon you, and learn of me; . . . For my yoke is easy, and my burden is light" (Matt. 11:29–30).

When you feel you can do no more, temporarily lay your challenges at His feet. . . .

Submitting "cheerfully and with patience" to all His will lets you learn precious if difficult lessons and eternal truths that will yield blessings (see Jacob 4:10).[1]

Some healing is gradual and some is instantaneous. And some healing can be an outright gift from the Father. I am grateful to have experienced all of them.

## "I Feel Pretty, Oh So Pretty!"

I was blessed to receive an outright gift of healing that was an incredible experience. But first, you have to understand some of the back story. Over the years, I have sung that song from *West Side Story*—"I feel pretty, oh so pretty!" and have laughed. I felt anything *but* pretty. I have spent my entire life feeling unattractive.

To be truthful, I was somewhat taught that I was not pretty. I had heard a litany of comments from various people in my life: "You'll never be beautiful, so work on your personality." Or, "Your friend is pretty and you are smart. That's just the way it is." I heard one of my personal favorites when I was a young adult and considering serving a mission: "You're not ugly enough to go on a mission." Excuse me? Ugly? Enough? Uh, OK . . . By the time I was an adult, my view of my exterior was set. No amount of compliments from my husband could change it.

When I was diagnosed with breast cancer and told I had to have a mastectomy, I thought, *You've got to be kidding me. Aren't I ugly enough?* The thought of losing my hair, which I felt was my one saving grace, hit me hard. I shall never forget the day when I was on my prayer walk and I realized that by the end of the month I would be bald. Completely bald. Ugly. I wondered if I could emotionally survive.

That day I prayed to Heavenly Father and asked for the gift of healing of my feelings about my appearance. Now, I'd been praying for complete healing for a while, but I knew going bald was not something I could survive very well emotionally on my own. I was tired of feeling ugly for fifty years of my life. I wanted healing. And I knew the only way to get it was to get it from God. So I asked.

And a strange thing began to happen. Day after day I felt prettier. I know it's strange and hard to explain, but I just felt prettier. I began to notice things about myself that I liked and were attractive.

And then came the day to face the mirror after my surgery. The bandages were off. And you know what, it was OK. It was different, but it was OK. I knew that I would eventually have reconstructive surgery, but in the meantime, it was fine. And look at my wonderful body! It was a miracle!

Next came the day when my hair started really falling out. I called my son Brennan and asked if he would come over on his lunch hour and buzz it all off. I buzzed his hair, and then he buzzed mine. As he was working away, he commented, "It's not every day you get to buzz off your mother's hair!" When he was done, we took pictures and he said I now looked like one of the Boyack brothers. (All four sons have had many "buzzes" in their lifetimes.) I went in the shower and shaved off all my hair right down to the skin.

Then I had to face the mirror. And an amazing thing happened. I looked in that mirror and I saw beauty. My eyes that I had always hated were shining. My skin was glowing. I had a good head! And a big smile. I realized I was truly beautiful.

I told my husband that I felt more beautiful in the last two months than I had ever felt in my life. He laughed and said it must have been the hair!

But I knew something deeper had happened. God healed my feelings about my appearance. I was finally able to see myself as He sees me—a marvelous work of art. And the voices I carried in my head for decades have been completely silenced. It was a gift from Him—pure and simple.

I learned an important lesson from this experience. God creates beauty. It's that simple. And when He created me, He created a lovely and pretty and down-right-*cute* daughter. I also realized that every single one of us is beautiful. Yes, we all have inner beauty, but I have discovered that every single one of us in all our shapes and sizes and ages and conditions, are truly beautiful on the outside too. That was something I had not understood before.

God creates beauty. God created me. God created you. And He did a good job on all of us.

## A Healing Blessing

I've also experienced healing as an instantaneous blessing. It was a really bad time. I had finished chemo, but was suffering with bronchitis and head-to-toe hives plus menopause. I didn't sleep at all for an entire month. I was a mess. The stake president had asked me to give a talk and the Friday morning before conference, I woke up and began to pray. I had hardly greeted Heavenly Father when I literally felt a spiritual prompting so strong and clear: "You need a blessing."

"What?!"

"You need a blessing. Get one today."

I thought to myself, *Blessing? I don't need a blessing. I had a blessing before my surgery and another before my chemo. I really don't need another one.*

The prompting came again. "You need a blessing, today."

"Fine, fine," I muttered. I went to talk to my husband. "Honey, I have no idea why but I'm supposed to have a blessing. Would you call the bishop and ask him to join you?" He said he would.

Later in the day, the bishop came by. I had been a bit stressed all day. I was bald. How would a blessing be handled? I fretted a bit and then thought, *Whatever. I will do whatever it takes.*

The bishop and my husband stood by my chair. The bishop asked me, "What would you like me to bless you with?"

I thought for a moment. "Well, I would really like to be able to take a deep breath without it hurting," I said. "And I would like to stop itching."

Then came the moment. My husband held the vial of oil over my head. He hesitated. "Uh, what should we do?"

"We anoint on the crown of the head," said the bishop.

"Brace yourself!" I said and whipped off my headscarf. I felt the slightest flinch from the bishop. But, bless his heart, he continued on. He blessed me once again that I was being completely healed through my faith. And then he blessed me that I would be

123

able to breathe from that moment on and that the itching would stop in that moment. He then gave me a beautiful blessing relative to the talk I was about to give.

Instantaneous healing. I was immediately able to take a deep breath without pain, and the pain never came back. After a month of itching head to toe, my skin and body were quiet. The allergic reaction was commanded to cease, and it did.

I have never before experienced such an immediate blessing. I gained a testimony that such healing is possible through the power of the priesthood and our faith.

## Healing the Heart

Some healing is more gradual and takes time. That was my experience with healing my heart. It had taken a beating and was still ticking, but it was certainly hurting. My emotions were raw. My sense of humor was noticeably absent. I felt numb. Completely, emotionally numb. It was such a strange feeling. I didn't get upset about stuff anymore because I was just too tired. It wasn't that I didn't care. I was just completely exhausted.

I knew I needed the healing of the Savior. His was the only balm that would soothe my wounded soul.

I began to pray daily for this healing—this deep soul healing—that I knew I needed. It came—but ever so gradually. And it is still coming.

One thing that really helped heal my heart was being able to go to the temple again.

When I was diagnosed, I came face to face with death. In that moment, only one thing was important to me. The covenants and ordinances of the temple which bound me to the Lord for eternity and which have bound my family to me. Those sealing ordinances were *everything*.

I didn't care about my house, my car, or any material things whatsoever. I didn't care about my resume of accomplishments or list of activities.

I didn't care about *anything* but my family and my testimony and the ordinances and blessings of the temple. I could face death calmly, knowing those were in place.

While I was sick, I longed to return to the temple and enjoy the unique peace and healing found within its walls.

When I was finally well enough to go for a short visit, I decided to do the initiatory ordinance. I bought a white cap to cover my bald head and went to the temple. I cried through the whole thing, as did all the ordinance workers. The words of those sacred blessings took on new meaning for me that day. What a joy it was to be back in the house of the Lord and hear those blessings. The temple truly is a house of healing.

Elder Richard G. Scott had a similar experience with the temple after the death of his wife. He states:

> Fourteen years ago I decided to attend the temple and complete an ordinance at least once a week. When I am traveling I make up the missed visits in order to achieve that objective. I have kept that resolve, and it has changed my life profoundly. I strive to participate in all the different ordinances available in the temple.
>
> I encourage you to establish your own goal of how frequently you will avail yourself of the ordinances offered in our operating temples. What is there that is more important than attending and participating in the ordinances of the temple? What activity could

have a greater impact and provide more joy and profound happiness for a couple than worshipping together in the temple? . . .

What I am trying to teach is that when we keep the temple covenants we have made and when we live righteously in order to maintain the blessings promised by those ordinances, then come what may, we have no reason to worry or to feel despondent.[2]

I would echo Elder Scott's testimony. Are you experiencing trials? Do you desire healing? Go to the temple. Go regularly. Whatever that means for you—whether it's monthly, twice a month, or weekly. Go by yourself. Go as a couple. Don't let anything stand in your way. Just go. When you do, you will be armed with power and the angels will have charge over you and your children. Your family will be together for eternity. You will have a source of healing that will bless your life in countless ways.

## The Gift of Humility

Even in trying times, we can receive great gifts. For decades, I had desired a gift of understanding which had not come. I admired the people in my life who were humble. Truly humble. They were successful by the world's standards, and yet they were not the slightest bit arrogant or prideful. They radiated love, meekness, and humility that I knew was a core part of their being.

I did not understand how to get there. I had fought for many years to reach a point of strength and confidence. But when I got there, I didn't know how to take the next step. How does a person have strength and yet also have a humble heart? I knew I had "I" problems and I could not figure out how to cure them. I had watched these humble people for years and prayed for understanding on how I could be like them. I worked to eliminate the pride issues in my life, but somehow couldn't figure out how to acquire such Christlike humility.

And then my challenges and experiences started. As they began to multiply, I began to ponder and study the description of humility I found in the scriptures:

> For the natural man is an enemy to God, and has been from the fall of Adam, and will be, forever and ever, unless he yields to the enticings of the Holy Spirit, and putteth off the natural man and becometh a saint through the atonement of Christ the Lord, and becometh as a child, submissive, meek, humble, patient, full of love, willing to submit to all things which the Lord seeth fit to inflict upon him, even as a child doth submit to his father. (Mosiah 3:19)

I knew this scripture held the key for me to understand humility. What I have come to realize is that a child submits to his father because he loves his father. And he knows for a surety that his father loves him. The child submits because he knows that everything his father does is in his best interests.

As each successive trial came and increased my burdens, I groaned under the weight of it all. Day after day, I bowed my head in submission to my Lord. Day after day, I turned my life over to Him who atoned for me personally. Day after day, I relied on His love.

Each new experience brought new pain, new suffering. But each experience also brought the comfort of the Holy Ghost and the promptings to yield to the will of the Lord. Each time I was encouraged to let go of the control. Let go of the fear. And trust, just completely trust.

I realized that my heart was changing.

Each experience demanded that I once again dig deep. I knew

my Heavenly Father knew me and loved me. I knew my Savior did as well. I knew that every single experience they had designed for my earthly experience was for my good and were motivated by love for me.

And as the trust and love came, I chose to be submissive and humble. Not only was I willing to endure the will of the Lord, it became my desire. I wanted His will to be done in my life. Even if that meant that I would endure pain and experience traumatic things, I wanted His will to be done. No matter what.

I learned it's hard to be prideful when your entire life is disintegrating around you. I began to understand much more deeply the struggle and suffering of others. Each day was an effort to survive, and as the trying times continued, I realized that everyone else was trying to survive as well. We were all trying to do the best we could. I stopped making comparisons; I was no different and no better. I was the same. More than that, I had no desire to be better than anyone. I was filled with love and compassion for those around me. I wanted to help them and needed their help in return. Meekness and teachableness took on new clarity.

I am now beginning to understand the attributes of a child—submissive, meek, humble, patient, full of love, willing to submit.

It's not about me anymore. It's all about the Lord.

## Learning to Let Go

A huge part of the healing and the humility was learning to let it go. I kept hearing Susan's voice in my head, "Let it go. Let it go." God has said it in His way, "Therefore, let your hearts be comforted concerning Zion; for all flesh is in mine hands; be still and know that I am God" (D&C 101:16). Those words have echoed through my mind and heart all year.

I once received a plaque with some "Be" phrases on it and I read those with interest. Be smart. Yup. Be grateful. Oh, yeah. I read on down the list until I came to the tough one: "Be still." That was the one I needed to work on.

As I've been going through everything, I had a joke I would tell.

God commanded Merrilee to be still. SMASH. Prop 8.

God commanded Merrilee to be still. CRASH. Breast cancer.

God commanded Merrilee to be still. PULVERIZE. Unemployment.

Angel reports to God, "Well, I think she's still now. . . . Yeah, she's not moving."

In the middle of my trying times, I learned an important lesson about letting go. One day I went to my radiation doctor, who asked how I was doing, and I had a complete meltdown. I went to the next doctor, my oncologist, who asked me the same question, and I melted down again! I was sick in the grocery store. Then I had to go to the dentist for a routine cleaning.

The dentist looked carefully at my teeth and pulled out his fancy camera wand. He showed me the giant image of one of my crowns on a tooth. He said, "Look, this crown is cracked from one end to the other right down the middle! I've never seen that happen in all my years of practice!"

My crown was cracked.

Boy, if that was ever a metaphor for my life! Indeed, I was feeling that my Eternal Crown was severely cracked as well.

I just went home and went to bed. There was no use! It seemed as though every single part of my life was cracking. Every single day brought new and huge challenges.

The next morning when I woke, I didn't even get out of bed before I had a long talk with Heavenly Father. I didn't dare! I told Him that I could not handle the things that were coming my way. I told Him that I knew that the Savior had borne my suffering and could help me endure these burdens. I knew that it was the only way.

New resolve filled me. Somehow, I decided that I had cried enough, complained enough, and wondered enough. It was time to have absolute, unwavering faith in my Savior. It was the only way I would be able to survive.

This has indeed been a year of letting go. A time of stillness. And in that stillness I have learned much. Author Emily Freeman wrote:

> In the midst of tribulation . . . [t]he mind searches for explanation; the heart questions its ability to withstand such intense emotion. In the search for a definite answer hope becomes dim and the struggle to simply exist takes over. . . . We beg to understand the reason for the suffering.
>
> We do not experience trials just to see if we will make it through. Each of us experiences the refiner's fire for one reason—to come to know the Refiner. We are not just tried; we are proven. Priceless lessons can be learned from the Master during times of adversity. It is in these moments of heartache that we come to know the Savior and more fully appreciate His atoning sacrifice.[3]

I truly have come to know the Savior. I have come to rely on Him. I have prayed that His atoning sacrifice would heal my heart and my body and my soul. And my prayers have been answered.

The Savior is the only one who can repair my cracked crown and make it perfect and stronger than ever. My Eternal Crown is granted to me only by His grace and His atonement on my behalf. He offers the same blessings to us all.

## CHAPTER 10

# Choosing to Move Forward

E arly in the path of my trials, I thought that I was going to end up only needing a lumpectomy. The doctors all assured me of that and I thought as I prayed that that would the path for me. I felt sure of it. But as things progressed, the medical tests revealed that my cancer was more extensive and that I was going to have to have a mastectomy. I remember meeting with the surgeon and the radiologist where they both confirmed that I would indeed need to have a mastectomy.

I made it all the way to the parking lot.

Yes, the news was devastating from a physical standpoint. It was going to be a whole lot more painful and a whole lot more involved than a simple lumpectomy. But what was truly devastating to me was that I thought I had received an answer to prayer. And it was not turning out that way. So what went wrong?

The questions began to ping-pong around my head. Had I

not heard the Spirit correctly? Who was I listening to, then? What had I done wrong?

And, of course, for a very brief nanosecond, I thought, *Didn't God answer my prayers?* But I knew beyond any doubt that God was aware of me and my situation and that He answered my prayers. Clearly, then, the problem was with me.

The spiritual crisis began. If I hadn't heard that answer correctly, what else had I not heard correctly? What else had I messed up?

I took a prayer walk along the road with these agonizing questions reverberating through my soul. What about everything that I thought had been inspiration? Had I been mistaken? I walked until I reached the church.

It was early on a weekday so no one was there. I went into the chapel and sat in the dark and poured out my soul to God. Where had I gone wrong? Why hadn't I heard correctly? How was I to move forward with so much doubt about my ability to hear? I felt that I was deaf and blind. I prayed.

Finally, I left and began the long walk home. I was quiet. After a time, I thought, *Well, I don't know everything. And I will make mistakes. But this much I do know. I know that my Heavenly Father lives. I know that He knows exactly who I am and that He loves me. I know that my Savior lives and that He loves me and heals me. I know the Church is true and that the prophet is God's prophet. I know that I have love in my life—my husband, my children, my family, my friends.*

*This is all I know. But I do know that. Each day I will just choose to do good and be good. One day at a time and one step at a time. I will choose to be faithful.*

The tears stopped and I was filled with conviction. I still felt like I was wandering in the dark, unable to see or hear. But I *knew* what I knew. When all is shaken, you dig down until you find the truth. I knew what I knew.

Trials are hard for a reason. Sometimes our trials shake us to the depths of our soul. What do we do then?

## We Can Stand Our Ground

The Lord states,

> For he will give unto the faithful line upon line, precept upon precept; and I will try you and prove you herewith. . . . Therefore, be not afraid of your enemies, for I have decreed in my heart, saith the Lord, that I will prove you in all things, whether you will abide in my covenant, even unto death, that you may be found worthy. (D&C 98:12, 14)

Will I be found worthy? Will I abide in His covenant? Will I be faithful to my baptismal and temple covenants? Will my devotion to my Savior, His gospel, and the plan of salvation remain true no matter what?

The answer for me is yes. True and faithful. No matter what. Elder Jeffrey R. Holland, speaks with understanding:

> I would ask all of us, in moments of fear or doubt or troubling times, to hold the ground we have already won even if that ground is limited and under attack. . . .
>
> When you are confronted with challenges that are difficult to conquer or have questions arise, the answer to which you do not know, *hold fast to the things you do know.* Hang on to your firmest foundation, however limited that may be, and from that position of strength face the unknown.[1]

Holding our ground and holding fast to what we do know becomes vital when we are so shaken that we have no idea which way is up. Indeed, these are the first steps. Once we stop, take stock in our situation, and take a firm stand, we can begin to step forward again. Remember, "All things are possible to him that believeth" (Mark 9:23).

## We Can Move Forward with Faith

All of us have experienced a time when we thought we received direction only to have things turn out differently. When the sale of our home fell through, I remember the look of confusion on my husband's face. "But we prayed about this!" he said, shaking his head. "We felt it was the right thing to do. Didn't we hear Him right?" I chuckled softly and said, "Welcome to my world!" We discussed how we could have received an answer that was the correct course of action but that still resulted in something different than what we anticipated. Perhaps someday we would have the answers as to why. Perhaps not. But we had to keep moving forward in faith.

Anne Osborn Poelman refers to this experience as encountering our own personal "mists of darkness."

> There surely will be times in each of our lives when we can't see the pathway, when everything around us feels confused and uncertain. We will indeed be surrounded by our own personal "mists of darkness." During these challenging, unsettling times, it is essential to navigate by faith, relying on the guidance of the Holy Ghost. If in times of crisis you can't sense the celestial homing beacon, *recall the last time you felt that inspiration and, using that experience as a spiritual "marker buoy," extrapolate your course from there.*[2]

We need to stop, take our direction, and continue to faithfully move forward.

## We Can Rely on Our Testimony

President Thomas S. Monson related the tragic story of a sister who was escaping post-war Germany with her young children. As she traveled, her children died and she paused to bury each one—first with a spoon and then with her bare fingers. President Monson relates the end of the story:

> When she finally reached her destination of Karlsruhe, Germany, she was emaciated. Brother Babbel said that her face was a purple-gray, her eyes red and swollen, her joints protruding. She was literally in the advanced stages of starvation. In a Church meeting shortly thereafter, she bore a glorious testimony, stating that of all the ailing people in her saddened land, she was one of the happiest because she knew that God lived, that Jesus is the Christ, and that He died and was resurrected so that we might live again. She testified that she knew if she continued faithful and true to the end, she would be reunited with those she had lost and would be saved in the celestial kingdom of God.[3]

The holy scriptures testify, "Behold, the righteous, the saints of the Holy One of Israel, they who have believed in [Him], they who have endured the crosses of the world, . . . they shall inherit the kingdom of God, . . . and their joy shall be full forever" (2 Nephi 9:18).

This woman knew her core. She had reached the point where all seemed hopeless. All seemed lost. But in that moment, she stopped and solidified her core beliefs. God lives. Jesus is the

Christ. Life goes on. And it was only drawing on the strength of her deepest convictions that she was able to survive and carry on. True and faithful to the end. No matter what.

## We Are Strong

It is often when we are faced with trying times that we gain a testimony of our own personal strength. We all have strength, and we have always had it. It is unique and personal to us, but it is grounded in the truths we know. Those truths, and our commitment to those truths, give us our strength and our ability to withstand come what may.

A colleague of mine who was enduring the pain of her only son dying of cancer once said to me, "People say I'm strong. I'm not strong. You just do what you have to do." That idea has stayed with me ever since. You just do what you have to do. Frankly, I believe that *is* her strength.

Elder D. Todd Christofferson said,

> Exercising agency in a setting that sometimes includes opposition and hardship is what makes life more than a simple multiple-choice test. God is interested in what we are becoming as a result of our choices. He is not satisfied if our exercise of moral agency is simply a robotic effort at keeping some rules. Our Savior wants us to become something, not just do some things. He is endeavoring to make us independently strong—more able to act for ourselves than perhaps those of any prior generation. We must be righteous, even when He withdraws His Spirit, or, as President Brigham Young said, even "in the dark."[4]

I did not truly understand this principle until I found myself stumbling around in the dark. We must become strong—and realize the strength we do have—and keep doing what we have to do. As we do this, we will become who we are meant to be. We must be righteous and committed to truth and faith. We must exercise our true strength.

## We Have a Bright Future

Several months ago, I received a small package from my sister. She calls her gifts "hugs," and they were truly that as I was wading through difficult times. Inside the package was a small framed quote from Christopher Robin to his Pooh Bear. The quote has had a profound impact on me and resides on my desk to this day,

> Promise me you'll always remember . . .
> You're BRAVER than you believe,
> And STRONGER than you seem,
> And SMARTER than you think.[5]

I know that is true for you as well as for me. You *are* braver than you believe. Look at all you have survived! It's incredible! You *are* stronger than you seem. You have seen what you have done and who you have become. And you *are* smarter than you think. You have faced life with creativity and endurance and have solved many, many problems that seemed insurmountable.

President Thomas S. Monson offered encouragement in a dark time with these words,

> I testify to you that our promised blessings are beyond measure. Though the storm clouds may gather, though the rains may pour down upon us, our knowledge of the gospel and our love of our Heavenly Father and of our Savior will

comfort and sustain us and bring joy to our hearts as we walk uprightly and keep the commandments. There will be nothing in this world that can defeat us.

My beloved brothers and sisters, fear not. Be of good cheer. *The future is as bright as your faith.*[6]

Those stirring words can be a beacon to individuals as well as for the entire church. A beacon of hope. The future *is* as bright as your faith. As we dig deep to find our core faith, we will find the strength we need to endure, to learn, and to become. I know this is true. The future is as bright as *your faith*.

# We Are Loved

My journey is not over. I continue to wade through many trials. I am still in the middle of it. Your journey is not over either.

But I do know this. Heavenly Father loves us tenderly as a dear and loving parent. Our beloved Jesus loves us to a depth we will never comprehend. The gospel and the plan of happiness are true and real. The power of the priesthood is real. The temple is a gift.

I know that you, too, have these gifts available to you in your life. You are so much stronger than you'll ever know. You have powerful choices available to you that will help you. You have been reserved for the latter days to battle the Adversary, and you can and will prevail. Each of us has blessings available to us and guidance from the Spirit to help us nourish our soul. Each of us can choose to be true and faithful no matter what. You have experienced many strengthening experiences in your life, as have I.

I do not know everything. I don't have all the answers to "Why?" or "Why me?" or "Why now?" But I no longer need to know. My only desire is to have my will wholly absorbed in the will of the Lord. It is His will I seek. I know that His will is love—love for me, love for my husband, love for my family.

And He is always there. He encircles us in the arms of His love.

This much I do know—in trying times, just keep trying!

# Epilogue

In the few months since I finished writing this book, my life has continued on an interesting path. I have completed both of my reconstruction surgeries, and I'm now home healing and working some more on that whole commandment to "Be still."

One last story to share: After six hours of surgery (I had the TRAM procedure for those who are interested), the nurses had just transferred me to my bed in the hospital when my husband's phone rang. He jumped up and almost mowed down the nurses as he made a beeline for the door so he could answer the call. On the other end of the line was a great job offer.

Now, don't you think God has dramatic timing? No one could have scripted that ending. It's almost as if He said, "OK, you two are done for now." It was truly a miracle. My husband told me later that I looked at him with my post-surgery, still-drugged eyes and said, "Inside, I am screaming with happiness. Inside, I'm doing a very gentle Dance of Joy. I'm so happy."

Epilogue

We are both healing. We do not know what the future holds and it will probably still be a while before we stop ducking for bullets. But for now, we are grateful that seven months of unemployment have ended. We are grateful that a year and a half of dealing with breast cancer is winding down. We are grateful to be alive.

As I move forward with my life with new lessons learned, I still seek only that the will of the Lord be done in my life. Good, bad, hard, or easy. That is all I desire.

# Acknowledgments

I'd like to thank Jana Erickson for her unfailing support, and I'd especially like to thank Lisa Mangum, who did an incredible job of editing. You're both amazing.

Thanks, too, to the whole Deseret Book team, including Shauna Gibby and Tonya Facemyer.

# Notes

## Chapter 2: Choosing to Stay True and Faithful

1. Henry B. Eyring, "Spiritual Preparedness: Start Early and Be Steady," *Ensign,* November 2005, 38, 40.

2. Neal A. Maxwell, "Jesus, the Perfect Mentor," *Ensign,* February 2001, 15.

3. Neal A. Maxwell, "'Swallowed Up in the Will of the Father,'" *Ensign,* November 1995, 24.

4. Joseph Smith, *History of The Church of Jesus Christ of Latter-day Saints,* 2d ed., 7 vols. Edited by B. H. Roberts (Salt Lake City: The Church of Jesus Christ of Latter-day Saints, 1948), 3:328–29; emphasis added.

5. Neal A. Maxwell, *Lord, Increase Our Faith* (Salt Lake City: Bookcraft, 1994), 3.

6. Dieter F. Uchtdorf, "Prayer and the Blue Horizon," *Ensign,* June 2009, 6.

7. Thomas S. Monson, "Be of Good Cheer," *Ensign,* May 2009, 89.

8. Jeffrey R. Holland, "Lessons from Liberty Jail," in *BYU Magazine* (Winter 2009): 37; emphasis in original.

9. Maxwell, *Lord, Increase Our Faith,* 3.

10. William Fowler, "We Thank Thee, O God, for a Prophet," in *Hymns of The Church of Jesus Christ of Latter-day Saints* (Salt Lake City: The Church of Jesus Christ of Latter-day Saints, 1985), no. 19.

11. Jeffrey R. Holland, *Broken Things to Mend* (Salt Lake City: Deseret Book, 2008), 48.

## Chapter 3: Choosing to Be Positive and Grateful

1. Joseph Smith, *History of The Church of Jesus Christ of Latter-day Saints,* 2d ed., 7 vols. Edited by B. H. Roberts (Salt Lake City: The Church of Jesus Christ of Latter-day Saints, 1948), 3:329.

2. Jeffrey R. Holland, "Lessons from Liberty Jail," in *BYU Magazine* (Winter 2009): 39; emphasis added.

## Chapter 4: Choosing to Learn and Grow

1. Ronald E. Osborn, http://www.quotemountain.com.

2. Henry B. Eyring, "Education for Real Life," *Ensign,* October 2002, 18–19.

3. Personal correspondence with author.

4. Personal correspondence with author.

5. Eyring, "Education for Real Life," 18–19.

6. Henry B. Eyring, "Real-Life Education," *New Era,* April 2009, 5.

## Chapter 5: Choosing to Fight and Win

1. Gary Lawrence, "Wonder What the War in Heaven Was Like? Watch California this Fall," *Meridian Magazine,* http://www.meridianmagazine.com/ideas/080711war.html; emphasis in original.

2. James J. Hamula, "Winning the War against Evil," *Ensign,* November 2008, 50.

3. Brigham Young, in *Journal of Discourses,* 26 vols. (London: Latter-day Saints' Book Depot, 1854–1886), 1:116.

4. Henry B. Eyring, *Because He First Loved Us* (Salt Lake City: Deseret Book, 2002), 19.

5. Greg Wright, *Satan's War on Free Agency* (Orem, Utah: Granite Publishing, 2003), 76; emphasis in original.

6. D. Todd Christofferson, "Moral Agency," *Ensign,* June 2009, 49.

7. Eyring, *Because He First Loved Us*, 80.

8. Boyd K. Packer, "Revelation in a Changing World," *Ensign,* November 1989, 15, 16.

9. Emily Freeman, *21 Days Closer to Christ* (Salt Lake City: Deseret Book, 2007), 63; emphasis in original.

# Chapter 6: Choosing to Love, Listen, and Fill Our Lives with Light

1. Henry B. Eyring, *Because He First Loved Us* (Salt Lake City: Deseret Book, 2002), 65.

2. Greg Wright, *Satan's War on Free Agency* (Orem, Utah: Granite Publishing, 2003), 56.

3. Kevin W. Pearson, "Faith in the Lord Jesus Christ," *Ensign,* May 2009, 40.

4. Personal correspondence with author.

5. Joseph Smith, *Teachings of the Prophet Joseph Smith,* sel. Joseph Fielding Smith (Salt Lake City: Deseret Book, 1976), 76.

6. Pearson, "Faith in the Lord Jesus Christ," 40; emphasis in original.

7. #49, *The Wizard of Oz,* DVD, directed by Victor Fleming (1939; Burbank, CA: Warner Home Video, 2009).

8. Julie B. Beck, "Fulfilling the Purpose of Relief Society," *Ensign,* November 2008, 111.

9. James J. Hamula, "Winning the War against Evil," *Ensign,* November 2008, 52; emphasis added.

10. Neal A. Maxwell, *Lord, Increase Our Faith* (Salt Lake City: Bookcraft, 1994), 110.

11. Dieter F. Uchtdorf, "Prayer and the Blue Horizon," *Ensign,* June 2009, 5.

12. Jeffrey R. Holland, *Broken Things to Mend* (Salt Lake City: Deseret Book, 2008), 133–34.

13. Robert D. Hales, in Conference Report, April 2002, 80–81.

14. Holland, *Broken Things to Mend,* 135.

15. Richard G. Scott, "Trust in the Lord," *Ensign,* May 1989, 37.

16. Eyring, *Because He First Loved Us,* 30.

# Chapter 7: Choosing to Nourish Body and Soul

1. Russell M. Nelson, "Four Steps to Learning," *Tambuli,* September 1989, 39.

2. Douglas L. Callister, "Our Refined Heavenly Home," *Ensign,* June 2009, 55.

3. Sheri L. Dew, at the World Congress of Families V in Amsterdam, Netherlands, 10 August 2009; http://www.ldschurchnews.com/articles/57746/Sheri-L-Dew-The-Power-of-Virtue.html; emphasis in original.

4. Gordon B. Hinckley, *Standing for Something* (New York City: Random House, 2000), 45.

5. Dieter F. Uchtdorf, "Happiness, Your Heritage," *Ensign,* November 2008, 118–19.

6. Larry Barkdull, *Gifts: True Stories of God's Love* (Salt Lake City: Deseret Book, 2004), 3.

## Chapter 8: Choosing to Celebrate the Good

1. Douglas L. Callister, "Our Refined Heavenly Home," *Ensign,* June 2009, 55.

2. Callister, "Our Refined Heavenly Home," 55.

3. Pablo Picasso, quoted in Ashton Applewhite, Tripp Evans, Andrew Frothingham, *And I Quote* (New York: St. Martin's Press, 1992), 389.

4. Berthold Auerbach, quoted in *Wisdom for the Soul,* compiled and edited by Larry Chang (Washington, D.C.: Gnosophia Publishers, 2006), 519.

5. Callister, "Our Refined Heavenly Home," 56, 57.

6. Sally Peterson Brinton, "Blessing Your Home with Music," *Ensign,* March 1983, 37–38.

7. Mark J. Nielsen, "The Wonder of the Creation," *Ensign,* March 2004, 60–61.

## Chapter 9: Choosing to Let Go and Heal

1. Richard G. Scott, "To Be Healed," *New Era,* April 2002, 5–6.

2. Richard G. Scott, "Temple Worship: The Source of Strength and Power in Times of Need," *Ensign,* May 2009, 43, 45.

3. Emily Freeman, *21 Days Closer to Christ* (Salt Lake City: Deseret Book, 2007), 115–16.

## Chapter 10: Choosing to Move Forward

1. Jeffrey R. Holland, *Broken Things to Mend* (Salt Lake City: Deseret Book, 2008), 140–41; emphasis in original.

2. Anne Osborn Poelman, *The Simeon Solution* (Salt Lake City: Deseret Book, 1994), 16–17; emphasis in original.

3. Thomas S. Monson, "Be of Good Cheer," *Ensign,* May 2009, 92.

4. D. Todd Christofferson, "Moral Agency," *Ensign,* June 2009, 53.

5. See "I'll Always Be with You," *Pooh's Grand Adventure: The Search for Christopher Robin,* DVD, directed by Karl Geurs (Burbank, CA: Walt Disney Home Entertainment, 2006).

6. Monson, "Be of Good Cheer," 92; emphasis added.

# About the Author

Merrilee Boyack is a popular speaker at BYU Education Week and at Time Out for Women conferences. She is an estate-planning attorney who conducts her part-time law practice from her home in Poway, California, where she also serves as a member of the city council. Merrilee and her husband are the parents of four sons.

# Also by Merrilee Boyack

## Toss the Guilt and Catch the Joy

### A Woman's Guide to a Better Life